Presenting the Past

Jill Liddington lives in Mytholmroyd near Halifax and is an Honorary Research Fellow at Leeds University. She is the co-author of *One Hand Tied Behind Us: the Rise of the Women's Suffrage Movement* which quickly became a suffrage classic. *The Long Road to Greenham* won the 1990 Fawcett Book Prize and her most recent history is *Rebel Girls: Their Fight for the Vote* (2006).

In *Presenting the Past,* Jill Liddington tells the dramatic story of how the diaries and letters survived since Anne Lister's death in 1840. She recounts how the code, in which Anne recorded her lesbian affairs in her journals, was eventually deciphered.

Successive generations of historians and editors have selected and presented *their* version of the Anne Lister story. Taking the reader into the Archives in Halifax where the Shibden Hall papers are preserved, *Presenting the Past* offers the first critical reappraisal of these very different images of Anne Lister.

Portrait of Anne Lister, Shibden Hall

By kind permission of Calderdale Leisure Services

Presenting the Past

Anne Lister of Halifax (1791-1840)

Jill Liddington

Pennine Pens

Published 1994 by Pennine Pens
New edition 2010

ISBN 1 873378 02 5

Pennine Pens,
32, Windsor Road,
Hebden Bridge,
West Yorkshire,
HX7 8LF.
0422-843724

Contents

Illustrations

Front cover: miniature portrait of Anne Lister, probably 1806-1810. By kind permission of Calderdale Leisure Services. With thanks to Tony Sharpe and Kevin Kilroy.

Back cover: Drawing of Shibden Hall, 1836, by John Harper, showing what the Hall might have looked like (SH:2/M/2). By kind permission of Calderdale District Archives.

Acknowledgements

Anne Lister of Shibden Hall, Halifax (1791-1840): Her Diaries and the Historians first appeared in Issue 35 of the *History Workshop Journal,* spring 1993, and is published by kind permission of the *Journal*.

In the Calderdale Archives, Alan Betteridge and his staff have helped enormously: the Shibden Hall papers could not be in more professional or caring hands. I also thank the current Anne Lister scholars - Muriel Green, Dorothy Thompson, Helena Whitbread and Cat Euler - for sharing with me their enthusiasm and interest. Cat Euler and I presented a paper, 'Exploring the Anne Lister Labyrinth: Images and Strategies', in September 1992; although this article was written by then, I am grateful to Cat for discussions which helped shape the final draft. I would also like to thank for their support and comments Jane Rendall, John Hargreaves, Ros Westwood, Malcolm Chase, Val Smith, Julian Harber and the *Journal* editors - Jinty Nelson, Anna Davin and Bill Schwartz.

Anne Lister of Shibden Hall, Halifax (1791-1840): Re-reading the Correspondence first appeared in the *Transactions of the Halifax Antiquarian Society,* 1993, and is published by kind permission of the Society. For their comments I would particularly like to thank Muriel Green, John Hargreaves, Tom Steele, Ros Westwood, Cat Euler, Pat Hughes, Helena Whitbread, Julian Harber, Anna Davin and Calderdale Archives staff: Alan Betteridge, Pat Sewell and Ian Thomas.

For all their help with *Presenting the Past* I would like to thank Chris Ratcliffe and Elaine Connell. I'm particularly grateful to Chris for handling everything so smoothly and with such patience.

Preface to the 2010 edition

Since *Presenting the Past*, I have also written *Female Fortune: Land, Gender and Authority: the Anne Lister Diaries and Other Writings*, 1833-36 (Rivers Oram, 1998), and *Nature's Domain: Anne Lister and the Landscape of Desire* (Pennine Pens, 2003) which focused on Anne at Shibden in 1832.

Scholarly fascination with Anne Lister has certainly continued. However, for this second edition, I decided to leave the text very largely as it was fifteen years ago, beyond a few points of clarification and some minor corrections.

There has also been sustained public interest in Anne Lister. While radio and television have sometimes offered a simplified version of Anne that omitted her rich complexities, BBC2 is now producing two programmes for spring 2010 which promise a portrait of Anne Lister and her world that she herself would recognize.

Anne Lister of Shibden Hall

Her Diaries and the Historians

Anne Lister - scholar and heiress who later ran her own estate with entrepreneurial flair - was one of the most remarkable women of pre-Victorian England. Born in Halifax on 3 April 1791,[1] Anne was the eldest surviving child of Captain Jeremy Lister, footloose veteran of the War of American Independence. After a rural East Riding childhood, Anne attended an elite girls' boarding school in York; then from 1806 she spent most of her life in Halifax, a centre of the West Riding worsted industry. Her father was youngest son of the Listers of Shibden Hall, but his brothers either remained unmarried or their children did not survive infancy; and it was Anne who eventually inherited the Shibden estate with its farms and tenancies, mining and quarrying interests. An intrepid European traveller, her great ambition was to visit Russia and venture beyond Moscow. And this she did. With her companion Ann Walker, she set out in 1839 via St Petersburg, reaching the Caspian Sea and eventually Western Georgia. Bitten by a fever-carrying tick, Anne Lister died near K'ut'aisi in this remote Russian province in September 1840.[2] It took Ann Walker six months to bring the body back across Europe for burial in Halifax Parish Church.

Only very recently has it become clear Anne Lister was a lesbian; previously she was best known as a compulsive diarist. In 1806, when she was fifteen, Anne began keeping a brief journal. Then from 1817, aged twenty-six, she wrote this diary systematically, recording social and political gossip, the books and journals she read (and in which languages), the latest scientific and industrial developments, and her visits among a rich network of female friends. She even maintained this habit of meticulous daily entries right up to her death in Russia. Understandably, the Anne Lister journals have long fascinated Yorkshire historians; but they were only drawn to national attention in 1984 when a *Guardian* article, 'The two million word enigma', alerted readers to the coming Anne Lister bicentenary in 1991:

> If a researcher with considerable dedication and faultless eyesight began today and worked assiduously for the next seven years, he or she might just manage to produce a critical edition of Miss Lister's journals in time for the anniversary...
>
> There are, however, some snags. It's not just that Anne Lister's diary is long (24 volumes, 6,000 pages, two million words); she also had one of the most illegible hands known to history and some of the diary is in code. Many a curious amateur has beaten a path to the archives in Halifax Central Library only to retreat, thoroughly demoralised and half-blind, before deciphering a single page...

The *Guardian,* noting Anne Lister never married and suggesting she 'may well have been a lesbian', ended with the challenge: 'All we need now is the dedicated researcher to fill in the gaps. Any takers?'[3]

1991 and the bicentenary have come and gone. Three books on Anne Lister *have* been published. Helena Whitbread's *I Know My Own Heart* (1988) at last made the diaries accessible to a wider readership and established beyond doubt Anne's lesbianism, prompting interest among transatlantic historians of gender and sexuality. The second, Muriel Green's *Miss Lister of Shibden Hall* (1992), based upon Anne's letters, is a more traditional portrait. More recently, Whitbread's *No Priest but Love* (1992) further explored Anne's lesbian relationships. But there is still no critical edition.[4]

Why not? There are at least three good reasons. The twenty-four volumes turn out to be twenty-seven, and the two million words to be almost *four* million - of which roughly a sixth are in Anne's private code.[5] By comparison, Samuel Pepys' diary (1660-69) is merely a million-and-a-quarter words. Indeed, had Anne Lister written less, her journals would undoubtedly be better known. Though not as illegible as the *Guardian* suggested, her heavily-abbreviated handwriting and letter-by-letter code is indeed daunting. Skim-reading or pulling out coded passages is tempting: but probably for any serious study of Anne Lister, to read the diaries means to transcribe them (or at least large sections of them).

Second, the Anne Lister treasure trail is further complicated. For a critical edition needs to be embedded in the extensive archival material of which the journals comprise merely a fraction. If the diary and its code is the jewel in the crown, its setting is resplendent and massive. Nearly two thousand of Anne's letters survive. Yet all her personal manuscript material represents merely one eighth of the vast Shibden Hall collection, dating from the thirteenth century and preserved in Calderdale District Archives in Halifax.[6] Alongside lie other collections of local papers containing more small Anne Lister gems, and beyond Calderdale is yet more material. So anyone eager to research Anne Lister's life can quickly become swamped by documents.

Third, the coverage of the diaries ranges so very widely that it overflows the neat categories convenient to historians. They record how a young woman without access to university education sustained a systematic programme of classical and scientific study; how industrialization helped reshape class relationships in a West Riding community; how political power was exercised by minor landed gentry both before and after 1832; and they give uniquely frank and unrestrained insight into the web of affectionate female relationships Anne nurtured in Halifax, York and - as her European travels widened - further afield. But their great value to the historian is precisely that Anne Lister *did* cram in such a dazzlingly rich mix of reading, observation and activity into each day - and then went on to record it all in the pages of her journals.

During her lifetime, few people realized Anne was keeping such a disciplined, detailed diary (and she was certainly extremely wary about revealing even to friends the personal coded sections). But in the 150 years since her death, the journals have intrigued successive local historians; faced with such a daunting mass of material, each generation has - perhaps inevitably - left us their *own* version of Anne Lister. These inherited images often vie confusingly with one another. They make scant mention of how each editor arrived at their version (in particular, their criteria for selection and omission); and seldom acknowledge their predecessors. But until we can be clear what we already know about Anne Lister and her diaries, and be clear how we know it, further serious study remains problematic.

So here I offer an historiographical overview, telling the story of the perilous survival of the diaries after Anne's death, and of how earlier generations - descendants, antiquarians and librarians, curators and editors - filtered our picture of the past. The article offers a critical appreciation of how the succcssive images of Anne Lister have been presented, posing to each version similar questions - what was selected and why, what access there was to the code, and how balanced is the version of Anne that emerges. Next, I have selected three short sample sections of the original diaries for complete transcription and for comparison with these inherited images. Finally I raise some of the key questions important to historians keen to use the magnificent Anne Lister material.

The Shibden Hall Papers: A Victorian Melodrama

When Anne Lister died near remote K'ut'aisi in 1840, a distraught and bewildered Ann Walker somehow managed to transport not just the coffin but also the diaries back to Halifax. In 1834 Ann Walker, a neighbour in her mid-thirties, had been persuaded by Anne Lister to join her at Shibden Hall. Ann Walker now returned home there, for she had inherited a life interest.[7] (Anne Lister's will, drawn up in 1836, had bequeathed her entire estate to 'my friend Ann Walker' on the strict condition that if she married, her claim to the estate 'shall thenceforth cease . . . as if the said Ann Walker should have then departed this life'. With two York solicitors, Ann Walker now became a trustee - until death or marriage, when the estate would revert to a very distant male Lister relation from Wales, and so to his direct male heirs.) [8]

Further inheritance problems soon loomed. Within two years of Anne Lister's death, it appeared that the wealthy Ann Walker, long given to melancholy, was 'of unsound mind'. In 1843 Ann Walker's sister, with the Listers' solicitor Robert Parker, and a doctor friend who had a private asylum near York, devised a plan for Ann Walker's forcible removal from Shibden, assisted by the local constable who, the doctor explained, 'must certainly be convinced of Miss W's insanity'.[9] Ann Walker was indeed removed by carriage and Parker's memorandum the following day offers a graphic account of what Ann Walker's relatives discovered when they arrived at Shibden Hall. Every room was locked, including Ann Walker's Red Room. There were no keys, so they directed

> the Constable to open it which he did by taking it off the Hinges - the Room was in a most filthy condition, and on the side of the Bed were a Brace of loaded Pistols . . . The Shutters were closed - an old dirty candle stick near the Bed was covered with Tallow, as if the Candle had melted away on it . . . Papers were strewn about in complete confusion. In the Red Room were a [great] many Handkerchiefs shatted [?splattered] all over with Blood . . .[10]

Ann Walker was now designated 'a lunatic' and the Hall became occupied by tenant families. But her claim to the Shibden estate remained intact - which the Listers from Wales found very provoking.[11] Litigation between the Lister and Walker families degenerated into acrimonious squabbling in Chancery about money. The dispute dragged on almost until Ann Walker's death in 1854. [12] Indeed this extraordinary saga finds finds echo in the melodrama of early Victorian fiction: Charlotte Brontë's *Jane Eyre* (1847) with its mad woman secretly locked away in the attic; and Charles Dickens' complex 'Jarndyce and Jarndyce' legal suit in *Bleak House* (1853) which had dragged on so long 'that no man alive knows what it means'.[13]

Despite the trek back across Europe, disorder and decay, insanity and litigation, the Anne Lister diaries *had* survived. In 1850 her trustees had arranged for a calendar to be drawn up of the Shibden papers, presumably all lying higgledy-piggledy since the departure for Russia eleven years earlier. The ensuing schedule is a jumble of items held in private gentry hands rather than a professional archivist's listing. But down among ancient title deeds at item 206, bundled up unceremoniously in three paper parcels, are listed 'Diaries & Journals of Mrs Lister'.[14]

John Lister's Anne Lister

The Lister family from Wales moved north to take up residence in Shibden Hall in 1855. The embarrassing Walker interlude of the previous fifteen years was smoothed over, and the impression cultivated of centuries of unbroken Lister occupation.[15] Young John Lister, best known as first national treasurer of the Independent Labour Party (ILP), was born in 1847 and so was only eight years old when his family finally inherited the estate. Exactly how much of the real story was generally known at the time? Certainly, memories of older Yorkshire people kept alive tales of an eccentric, masculine Anne Lister;[16] possibly the Brontës in nearby Haworth had also known something of her.[17] But at a time when love between women seemed to have no name other than 'romantic friendship', the image passed from father to son was probably of a wilful, proud spinster.[18] A clue to John Lister's impression of Anne at this stage is a melodramatic novel, *The Mistress of Langdale Hall: A Romance of the West Riding* (1872), written by one of the guests at Shibden. The heroine is recognizably Anne:

> Her haughty head slightly bent . . . Maud Langdale stood on the terrace of the old Hall in the West-Riding, which owned her as its mistress . . . She never intended to marry; no man would ever lord it over her in Langdale.

The implausible plot hinged upon similar property and inheritance questions that had earlier challenged Anne Lister: but more conventionally, Maud altered her will to give a life interest to a young girl she had adopted.[19]

It was John Lister himself who eventually made the first serious attempt to present a portrait of Anne. His edited selections from the diaries were published in the *Halifax Guardian* between May 1887 and October 1892. A scholarly and complex man, John Lister had developed an interest both in local history and in Gladstonian Liberalism, becoming a town councillor and then a county councillor. He also spent much of the 1880s among his archives and produced this 200,000-word transcript, representing just five per cent of the original diaries,[20] and entitled 'Social and Political Life in Halifax Fifty Years Ago'. The *Halifax Guardian* proudly published it to coincide with Queen Victoria's jubilee, noting 'they throw great light on some features of the town in the year when Her Majesty ascended to the throne'. It opened with a vivid account of how during the 1837 general election Anne Lister and Ann Walker, though voteless themselves, exerted considerable political influence as landowners on their tenants:

> Sunday, 23rd July. - [With Ann Walker] to Hatter's street tenant, Hinton, till 2.32, about A's tenants: John Mallinson, Hartley, and Standeven. If A would be contented to let them split their votes? No! . . . Better give a plumper* for Wortley [the Blue candidate ie Tory], and then talk about staying. Hinton said he could get twenty votes for £100. 'Then', I said, 'tell some of our committee. I think there are twenty Blues who would be glad of the votes.'[21]

Over the next five and a half years John Lister presented in 121 gripping instalments Anne's life from 1816 (when he believed her diaries began); he systematically offered a series of small chronological themes - such as 'Lord John Russell's First Reform Bill' and 'Poachers transported'. These vividly illustrate Halifax's

* Halifax was a two member constituency and electors each had two votes; a plumper was a vote given to just one candidate and was therefore particularly valuable.

growth as a worsted mill town in the 1820s and 1830s, and the effect improved road, canal (and later rail) transport had upon local industry. For instance, John Lister's selections provide an excellent guide to the subtle relationship between extending the Calder and Hebble Canal up into Halifax and the price small-scale local mine-owners could obtain for their coal:

> Monday, April 14.th [1828] - My father and I, talking of the coals in the estate. All the upper bed is got, except some in the Lower Brook Ing and adjoining, which . . . now might be worth getting to burn for cinders for the steam-engines . . . Sale of coals not so good; so many come up the new canal to the town from . . . Leeds, etc, at 9s per dozen, and, say, 2s leading [transport], or 11s; native coal arc 7s per dozen at the pit, and 7s leading, or 14s.[22]

John Lister also shows how Anne weighed her various entrepreneurial interests - agricultural tenancies, town property, mines and stone quarries, canal and railway shares - to maximize her income so that besides supporting her household she could indulge her expensive tastes: 'improving' Shibden Hall and foreign travel. His edition also illuminates class relationships in a town industrializing fast but still surrounded by gentry estates: the prudent intermarrying among local oligarchies - farming with banking, business with Tory politics, the church and military with law - and the shift between the outer ring of families whose wealth still largely came from land and the growing professional and industrial urban elite.[23]

Beyond this, John Lister is less helpful. Sections become bogged down in indigestible genealogical and antiquarian detail, or are impossible to read without a large-scale map; and the reader seldom comes close to Anne Lister's personal motives and feelings. Friends like Mariana Lawton, whom Anne loved above all, suddenly appear without a word of introduction.[24] Indeed, all her relationships with other women remain distinctly shadowy.

It is likely that the nature of these relationships remained closed to John Lister for a long time because they were written in Anne's secret code. Then perhaps towards the end of his *Halifax Guardian* edition, John Lister was puzzling over the cipher with a Bradford antiquarian, Arthur Burrell. Burrell had borrowed a volume of the diaries and years later recalled how:

> Up to that time we knew nothing of the cipher alphabet. I distinctly remember taking a volume back to Shibden . . .and telling Mr Lister that I was certain of two letters, *h* and *e;* and I asked him if there was any likelihood that a further clue could be found. We then examined one of the boxes behind the panels and half way down the collection of deeds we found on a scrap of paper these words 'In God is my . . .'. We at once saw that the word must be 'hope'; and the *h* and *e* corresponded with my guess. The word 'hope' was in cipher. With these four letters almost certain we began very late at night to find the remaining clues.* We finished at 2 am . . . The part written in cipher - turned out after examination to be entirely unpublishable. Mr Lister was distressed but he refused to take my advice, which was that he should burn all 26 volumes. He was as you know an antiquarian and my suggestion seemed sacrilege, which perhaps it was.[25]

The coded passages presented 'an intimate account of homosexual practices among Miss Lister and her many "friends" ', and, Burrell added, this 'very unsavoury document' contained evidence 'that these friendships were criminal'.[26] We may wonder why Burrell and John Lister was so fearful of possible scandal. It is difficult to recreate the exact historical context; but in 1885 all male homosexual acts, traditionally punished harshly, had become completely illegal. Public opinion, as the 1895 trials of Oscar Wilde showed, was extremely hostile and the 1885 Act became known as the 'Blackmailers' Charter'. Lesbians were not directly affected, but sexologists' theories may have prompted a new self-consciousness about 'abnormal' women. Additionally, it seems likely that John Lister himself was homosexual, and so any discussion about 'an inherited diseased condition' may have caused him particular anxiety about

* Example of code: In God is my hope. 4\ ∩504=–40. 5+3

unkind publicity. (A convert to Catholicism, he stood successfully in 1892 as an ILP candidate in the town council elections and unsuccessfully in 1893 and 1895 for Halifax parliamentary constituency.)[27] Whatever our speculation about the fear of family scandal, it is very likely the diary originals went back behind the panels. Certainly a forty-years' silence followed.

Muriel Green's Anne Lister

It was this erudite late-Victorian version of Anne Lister's public face which was passed down to local history researchers. Scholarly John Lister became first president of the Halifax Antiquarian Society; but, disenchanted with twentieth-century politics, he grew despondent and isolated. Shibden's coal seams became exhausted and the estate seemed doomed to crumble till the 1920s it finally left the Lister family. John Lister died in October 1933, taking with him to the grave his knowledge of the coded diaries.

Halifax borough now became owners of Shibden Hall and so the vast jumble of family papers fell to the local council. The borough librarian Edward Green received permission to enter the Hall to see the archives - taking with him his young daughter Muriel, also on the library staff and the person now allocated the job of bringing order to chaos.

Sixty years later, Muriel Green could still recall that first visit: a policeman living-in to ensure nothing was stolen, the big trunkfuls of manuscripts and unsorted letters. After two years spent cataloguing John Lister's books, she began work on the letters, including of course the Anne Lister correspondence.[28] Fascinated, Muriel Green began to transcribe Anne's letters for her Library Association dissertation. She just dipped into the diaries to check points, tried to work out the code but failed, and otherwise concentrated on the letters.[29]

Three months later Edward Green, conscientiously tracking down missing volumes of the diary, managed to make contact with Arthur Burrell, now living in London. Finally out it all tumbled: the dramatic cracking of the code forty or fifty years earlier. Burrell warned Green of 'what old Halifax scandal knows about Miss Lister . . .if there should be surviving any descendants of her "friends" '; but early in 1937 he forwarded the key to the cipher 'as you are legal owners of the Ms', adding cautiously 'My copy of the clue will be burnt later, so that unless someone else holds a clue you will be the sole possessors'.[30]

In the wake of Radclyffe Hall's banned novel, *The Well of Loneliness* (1928) and the *Sunday Express* attack upon it, few people could afford to ignore public opinion. Edward Green let Muriel have a copy of the key to the code; but, his daughter recalled, he kept the original under lock and key in his library safe.

> I don't think my father knew much about Anne Lister, that she was a lesbian or anything. And I never mentioned it. We didn't talk about it in those days. It would have cast a slur on the good name of the Lister family if it were known then, so I didn't put it into my Letters at all. It doesn't come into the Letters really.

So silence about the diaries continued. When Muriel Green produced her 'The Shibden Hall Muniments' listing (very professional compared to the 1850 attempt), the Anne Lister diaries received only a brief entry as a subset of the Lister letters.[31]

Green's substantial contribution to the historiography of Anne Lister is her systematic cataloguing and transcribing of the correspondence. Completed in 1938*, her thesis makes interesting comparison with John Lister's version. Muriel Green's Anne Lister is a librarian's portrait rather than an historian's; its focus is less Halifax and industrialization and more Anne's links with her increasingly aristocratic friends - in York, Paris and Russia. Consulting the earliest diaries as well, Green gives us the first real glimpse of Anne Lister's girlhood, capturing her sense of frustration with the reduced status of her own immediate family, compared to that of Uncle James at ancient Shibden and Uncle Joseph at elegant Northgate House in

* *Miss Lister of Shibden Hall* (1992) is a much slimmer edition of Green's 1938 dissertation.

Halifax. Green's edition of the letters also allows us to see how Anne played off one woman against another, deftly negotiating between the intimate private sphere and the formal public one.[32] But in the Radclyffe Hall era, it was prudent to present only the respectable face of Anne Lister, mistress of elaborate politenesses and flattering phrases. So, particularly where the letters have been heavily edited, our appetite is whetted about the more *private* Anne Lister of the diaries themselves and especially of the coded sections, the key to which remained locked in the library safe.[33]

Phyllis Ramsden's Anne Lister

Little more was published for the next twenty years (though the Halifax Antiquarians retained a watching brief).[34] Then in 1958 historian Dr Phyllis Ramsden, member of the borough education committee and wife of the chairman of the *Halifax Courier,* joined with her friend Vivien Ingham from London and set to work:

> It appeared likely to us that the Journals had never before been read in their entirety, and this we decided to do . . . Many passages, especially in the earlier volumes, were written in a cipher which we had to learn.[35]

It seems they did not know about the work of Muriel Green (who had left Halifax by then), and dismissed John Lister's mainly local focus as they themselves hoped to find 'material of more general interest'.[36] They began by asking the Halifax museums director (responsible for Shibden Hall where the diaries still lay) if they might borrow the original volumes to transcribe at home. They were allowed 'to borrow two volumes at a time', the director noting that 'it will naturally be necessary for my Committee to give approval should you wish to publish any of the material'. But he added helpfully 'I think we will be able to provide you with a key to the coded passages, should you require this' - undoubtedly Arthur Burrell's copy.[37]

Over the few years both Ramsden and Ingham read each of the

main run of twenty four volumes (the earliest three seem to have gone adrift again), and for each of these they produced a brief chronology of Anne Lister's activities together with summaries of the coded sections. These lists, compiled around 1966, offer the reader for the very first time a guide to the intimate passages which had so distressed John Lister. They open with the 1817 diary:

Mar 14	Aunt lends AL £5
Apr 24	conversation with Uncle Joseph abt future of Lister estates, & of her own current position at Shibden Hall
26	Mariana Lawton (M-) reports that her husband is being attentive to her
30	Father sends AL money. AL not quite open abt it to Aunt . . .
May 19	C- (M-'s husband) still v. against AL[38]

It is already absolutely plain exactly what Anne wanted to keep private in her laborious personal crypt: her sense of financial insecurity, plus the troubled triangular rivalry between Anne and Charles Lawton for the affection of Mariana, whose calculating marriage had so pained Anne. The summaries of later volumes show that while her love for Mariana continued, Anne's range of relationships broadened:

Dec 23	[1825]	flirting w.	Isabella Norcliffe
25		do	Mrs Milne
26		do	Miss Duffin[39]

Ramsden and Ingham expurgated certain coded passages - especially for the years when Anne Lister was in Paris: one six-month stay was summarized merely as 'almost exclusively of such purely personal content as to contain nothing of historic importance or interest' so 'the crypt passages have not been listed'.[40] In part they were bending to local censure. For in 1964 a new Halifax archive service had been created within the borough libraries department; and Ramsden and Ingham, keen to produce articles based upon the diaries, had written to the chief librarian requesting official permission to publish. Halifax Council's General Purposes Committee agreed in principle 'but referred the matter to the Town Clerk for guidance on certain matters'. Eventually this committee formally confirmed its permission but, added the chief librarian, this remained subject to a copy 'being submitted for the prior approval of the Libraries and Museums Sub-Committee':

> I may say that the Committee felt that this would be the best way to retain their right of ensuring that unsuitable material should not be publicised. When, therefore, you have any proofs ready, they may be sent either to the Town Clerk or to me for submission to the Committee.[41]

Here, then, is the clearest evidence of official attempts to suppress public knowledge of the coded sections of the diary - for fear of bringing down scandal upon an ancient local family - and perhaps upon the very town itself. For it was not till 1967 that a Sexual Offences Act finally decriminalized male homosexual acts, and only very gradually did this new liberalism begin to spread to small towns. Lesbianism, while directly affected by neither the 1885 Act nor the 1967 reform, remained hedged around by prejudice, secrecy and shame.

Ramsden and Ingham responded to this censorship by shifting their focus - to Anne Lister's travel. But Ingham continued to believe the coded sections important. In 1969, shortly before her death, she gave an impressive paper, 'Anne Lister in the Pyrenees', in which she bravely maintained 'many details of general interest are to be found in the shorter [coded] passages and no one with pretensions to serious study of the Journal can entirely ignore them'. Ramsden, who continued the work on her own after Ingham's death, was much more circumspect.[42] In her authoritative paper to the Halifax Antiquarians in 1970, 'Anne Lister's Journal (1817-1840)', she insisted that with very few exceptions the

> long accounts in crypt-writing of her sentimental exchanges with her friends, excruciatingly tedious to the modern mind

> . . . are of no historical interest whatever . . . It is notable that at all periods when the author was engaged in pursuits which she found mentally or physically satisfying the amount of 'crypt' falls to insignificance. [43]

Ramsden's paper nevertheless represents a major landmark in Anne Lister research. She was the first scholar with a detailed knowledge of the entire diaries who could place them in their broad historical context. She tried to write a book on Anne the traveller but, perhaps demoralized at not finding a publisher, eventually gave up. Her book-length accounts of Anne's ambitious travels to France, Denmark and Russia remain only in typescript, though do occasionally succeed in capturing Anne Lister and her era:

> When peace was finally declared in 1815 there was a perfect stampede of penned-up British citizens across the Channel . . . Anne Lister's whole youth had passed in the shadow of this great war. She was 24 when the battle of Waterloo was fought and her acquaintances in Halifax and York began to cross the Channel . . . At first her plans were geared entirely to catching up with her friends' experiences . . . [44]

But with few direct quotations to bring Anne to life, it all now reads rather ploddingly. Ramsden, ever respectful, decided to call 'her "Miss Lister" throughout, as she would expect of me, and to tell her story with restraint and decorum'; and keen to avoid parochialism, Ramsden misleadingly claimed 'Anne Lister had never had any close contact with politics'.[45]

As a result, Ramsden's typescripts remain just a quarry for researchers. Later, it seems that Ramsden, anxious lest people took short cuts to produce something of prurient interest, destroyed some of her material - probably including a transcript of the coded passages. Like John Lister before her, the tragedy is that Ramsden's painstaking years of work never reached a readership much beyond Yorkshire. However the 'Two million word enigma' *Guardian* article, which included an interview with Ramsden, did offer something of a final tribute - just eighteen months before her death in 1985.[46]

*   *   *

By then, public access to the Lister diaries had improved. From 1970 a new archivist introduced more professional policies and practices. 'Borrowing' the original diaries by the local elite was discontinued; the requirement to refer extracts for publication to a council committee fell into disuse; and in 1983 a revised 'Shibden Hall Muniments' list, drawing closely upon Muriel Green's work half-a-century earlier, properly expanded the Anne Lister entry and at last gave full details of the diaries - both the main run of 24 volumes and the three earlier ones. After almost 150 years, the journals had survived a perilous transmission process as dramatic as that of James Boswell diaries. Now, in the more liberal 1980s, they became available to all.[47]

Helena Whitbread's Anne Lister

Meanwhile, a few months after the *Guardian* article, Helena Whitbread (also from Halifax) came across the Anne Lister diaries in the Archives and began patiently deciphering the coded sections, later moving on to the handwritten sections.[48] Her hard work resulted in *I Know My Own Heart*, published in 1988 by Virago Press.

Now at last Anne Lister's extraordinary journals were opened up to national readership. Helena Whitbread's edition makes widely accessible the rich detail with which the diary is crammed: 'Betty Wood, the leech-woman of Northowram' who applied '6 leeches just under my right jaw' for over an hour to help Anne's swollen face; Anne's snobbery - as a Lister of Shibden Hall she expected tradesmen's daughters to *know* 'we never visited new people'; and her unconventional black clothes which included 'a pair of leather knee-caps to keep my knees warm when I am reading'.[49]

Whitbread's edition was bravely pioneering, openly recording for the very first time Anne's lesbianism, previously suppressed or merely hinted at. *I Know My Own Heart* tells of Anne's attempts to cure her venereal disease and suggests that Anne 'took her sexuality as God-given' and natural.[50] (Anne did not seek another bluestocking or independently-minded woman like herself: 'I am not an admirer of learned ladies. They are not the sweet, interesting creatures I should love.')[51] Yet lesbian relationships then had to be discreet. Whitbread reveals how Anne negotiated her way between the confessional private world of the coded passages and the public face of an accepted member of the Halifax gentry; this alone makes the Lister diaries such an invaluable source for historians.

Helena Whitbread's edition draws on the diaries from March 1817 to August 1824 and comprises about 115,000 words. The original diaries for this period total roughly 885,000 words; so *I Know My Own Heart: the Diaries of Anne Lister 1791 - 1840* represents a 13% selection of these seven-and-a-half years (or 3% of the whole diary). It was here that some reviewers grew concerned, suggesting:

> The sub-title is slightly ambiguous . . . The editor provides no explanation of how the code was 'cracked' . . . and ultimately the reader is left feeling rather too dependent on a selection of the diaries without sufficient explanation of how and why particular passages have been selected.[52]

Helena Whitbread's references to 'the unravelling of the coded entries' and her portrait of Anne Lister's network of sexual relationships with other women stirred local controversy. Some Halifax readers felt that the book's Introduction was disingenuous, given all the earlier work of John Lister and Phyllis Ramsden. Others held it overemphasized lesbian flirtations at the expense of Anne's broader intellectual and cultural interests. There was even alarm in certain antiquarian circles about publishing the private coded passages at all: what goes on in the bedroom should not make its way into the history books.[53]

Some of this criticism was just small-town prudishness which failed to appreciate that without Whitbread's courageous perseverance Anne Lister would not have found a readership much beyond Yorkshire. Indeed, most contemporary readers, especially those aware of lesbianism's problematic historiography, would warmly welcome Whitbread's pioneering edition. Certainly it has prompted wider interest in Anne Lister - including publication of Muriel Green's selection of the letters completed fifty years earlier; and Helena Whitbread's second volume of extracts, about Anne in Paris.[54]

Anne Lister's Original Diary

This then was the Anne Lister historiography as the 1991 bicentenary approached. Despite all perils, the journals *had* survived, the first three volumes reunited with the main run of twenty four. We also inherit the portraits of Anne Lister from Lister, Green, Ramsden and Whitbread: each version is very different - as if each generation, unhappy about what went before, bent the stick the other way. And in each case the methodology used as well as the criteria for selection and omission go unexplained, while debts to predecessors are scarcely acknowledged.

As the bicentary loomed, it seemed a full transcript of the diaries was sadly still some way off.[55] My own interest, originally alerted by the *Guardian* article, was really only sparked by *I Know My Own Heart*. From 1988 onwards I began to use Helena Whitbread's book in my own teaching, gradually adding other primary material and then pages of the original diaries. Then a Halifax Antiquarians' Society day school on Anne Lister in 1989 further roused my curiosity - especially about what previous editors had left out.[56] I decided to try and complete a full transcript onto disc; but when innocently preparing a funding application, my word count emerged - to my horror - not as two but *four* million words. Even just an 80% transcription demanded almost nine person-years! As costs soared the plan clearly grew too expensive.

However scholarly comment on this dilemma prompted me to reassess what historians could now practicably require:[57] not necessarily a complete transcript, but rather a critical appreciation of what was already known of the diaries, plus full transcription of short representative sections with an assessment of their value to the historian. Hence this article and its structure. For previous editors had implicitly adopted a thematic approach to the diaries; none had made available a complete transcript of sections. Given the recession, the entire diaries probably could not be transcribed; but at least this new structure would explicitly acknowledge the methodological difficulties faced by all those approaching them.

The remainder of this article therefore focusses on three short sections of the original diary; together they comprise a 58,500 word transcript, just 1.5% of the total diaries. I have made my selections aiming to reflect both the private and public faces of Anne Lister, as well as the major themes of her life.[58] The first of my three passages opens in 1806 when Anne was fifteen, revealing the evolution of her journal with its secret code. My second is from late 1819, selected because it covers both the national tensions surrounding Peterloo and developments of Anne's complex relationships. The third section comes from late 1832, chosen because it includes the first general election after the Reform Act and the courtship of Ann Walker. For each section I give the word length and proportion in code, together with the picture offered of Anne Lister and her world, comparing this with the versions presented by the earlier editors and assessing its overall value to historians.

Anne Lister 1806-1810

The earliest 'diary' is in fact a slender collection of loose fragile pages, covering the period from 11 August 1806 to 22 February 1810 (with some gaps) comprising roughly 20,000 words.[59] The context is the final years of the Napoleonic Wars and of George III's long reign. Jane Austen was writing her last three novels recording strict social and courtship conventions; and in the West Riding the young Brontë family was living nearby, before moving to Haworth. But while Howarth was an isolated hill village, Halifax was already a busy manufacturing town of a dozen streets clustered around its fine 1779 Piece Hall.

When the diary opens fifteen-year-old Anne is living with her parents, her younger sister Marian and schoolboy brothers Sam and John on the outskirts of Halifax. The very first entry clearly suggests why she started a diary:

> Monday August 11 Eliza left us. Had a letter from her on Wednesday morning by Mr Ratcliffe the 13th Inst.
> Wrote to her on Thursday 14th by Mr Lund.
> Wrote to her again on Sunday 17th - put into the Post Office at Leeds on the Monday following - that Evening the 18th had a parcel from her - Music, Letter & Lavender.

The journal begins unmistakably as a record of the relationship between Anne Lister and 'a girl of colour', Eliza Raine, wealthy daughter of an East India Company surgeon. They had met at York's fashionable Manor boarding-school where they shared a room.[60] Anne had left school, but Eliza was staying in Halifax during the summer before returning for a further year. Their intimacy was sustained over the next eight years by innumerable letters and by lengthy visits in Halifax, York and Scarborough.

The diary starts as a fairly brisk daily record, with less of the rich social detail or confessional asides of later volumes. Anne's studies with the scholarly Reverend Samuel Knight (later Vicar of Halifax) included algebra and geometry, rhetoric, Latin and Greek; she refers to it as a 'school' but it may have been more tutorials for individual pupils. She reads widely and even had a small 'study' containing a harpsichord - for Anne was an able musician, giving lessons to a Miss Alexander. She becomes drawn into the middle-class round of tea-drinking, card evenings and theatre visits. The diary gives rare glimpses of how Halifax perceived this unconventional young woman: a close friend reported back that a Mrs B-:

> was pleased with me - she said . . . 'I saw Miss Lister on Sunday'. 'Did you Ma'am?' Mrs B- 'What a pity that she does not pay more attention to her appearance, for those who do not know her judge from this, but you who see so much of her think nothing of it and indeed I do not wonder, for she is

> such a pleasant companion that I myself could have listened to her till I had forgot it.'[61]

This is as near as we come here to the public face of seventeen-year-old Anne Lister: an entertaining conversationalist, sometimes eccentricly dressed and, although she occasionally pretended otherwise, apparently with no romantic interest in men. Rather, she enjoyed sharing their intellectual and sporting interests, practising firing her father's pistols. On one occasion when he was away she fearlessly assumed his role:

> About 1/2 past [midnight] when Sam was in bed & I was just getting in, my mother came in a violent agitation to tell us that there was a man in the garret, & Mary a [servant] & he were asleep together on the bed. Upon this, Sam slipped on his breeches & shoes & I with nothing on but my night jacket over my Shift, my stockings & night cap on, took the pistols loadened with ball which were ready under my pillow & a sword - went with him & my mother upstairs - he took the candle - my mother scolded & threatened & I (though interceeding [sic] for the lad & Mary) stood ready to put into execution what seemed really necessary - after 1/4 of an hour we got the lad & Mary & Nancy into the Kitchen at last . . .[62]

Anne increasingly felt let down by her unreliable parents, preferring to spend time with her so-respectable uncles: Joseph Lister and his wife made her welcome at Northgate House, as did James Lister and his two unmarried sisters, Anne and Martha, at Shibden Hall just outside Halifax. But Anne Lister was already more complex a person than the high-spirited bookish tomboy they saw. The brief coded entries in the diary make this clear. Anne's first 'crypt' entry, October 1806, is in a Greek script she devised to note the date or time of day. Gradually she came to use this 'code' to record her correspondence with Eliza, her studies with Mr Knight, and - routinely - her menstruation. By 1808 this script - accessible to anyone with Greek - had evolved into the fairly impenetrable code which runs through the rest of Anne Lister's long diary.[63] *

* *The coded passages are distinguished here by being printed in italic.*

Why was this secret code developed? Anne probably devised it with Eliza Raine about the time of Eliza's visit to Halifax in late 1808.[64] An early entry in the new code in October hints at this: Anne and Eliza spent the evening with Miss Alexander with whom Anne flirted. 'Drank tea at Mr A's and supped also - after tea at Eliza's instigat[ion] I had Miss A *on my knee, kissed [her].*' When Eliza departed a fortnight later, Anne 'went to bed before tea *of grief at [her] departure*'; the code thereafter continues intermittently.[65]

In June 1809 Anne set off on a lengthy visit to Scarborough and then to York where a new sophisticated social world opened. Unfortunately there is then a sixth-month gap in this diary; but amazingly Eliza Raine's diary (July 1809 - November 1810) has also survived and is in the Shibden Hall collection. This records how the two girls visited Malton where their friend Isabella Norcliffe's family had its estate, and how in York 'Miss Lister & I were introduced at the Rooms'.[66] But Anne's visit ended abruptly in January 1810 when she learnt that her brother John was dangerously ill. She hurried back to Halifax and his bedside. (Before he died, John asked how she had got on at York and had perceptively commented 'I'm afraid they have spoilt you'.[67] Anne was much affected by his death.)

From then until the opening of the second volume in 1816, it is difficult to piece together from the diaries exactly how Anne Lister's relationship with Eliza developed and how her private code evolved. However, brief entries in Eliza's slender diary (using a code identical to Anne's) reveal that in August 1810 Eliza was again in Halifax; she regularly visited the Listers at Ellen Royd on the edge of the town, and she and Anne developed all the intimacy of a marriage:

Sunday 5 Dined at Ellen Royd . . .
9 I dined at Mrs J. Lister's & heard an account of the amiable I[sabella] N[orcliffe] . . .
14 *Dear L & I had a reconciliation . . .*
16 *. . . L & I had a difference which happily was made up before the conclusion of the day but left me e[x]ceedingly ill*
17 *. . . my husband came to me & finally a happy reunion was accomplished.*[68]

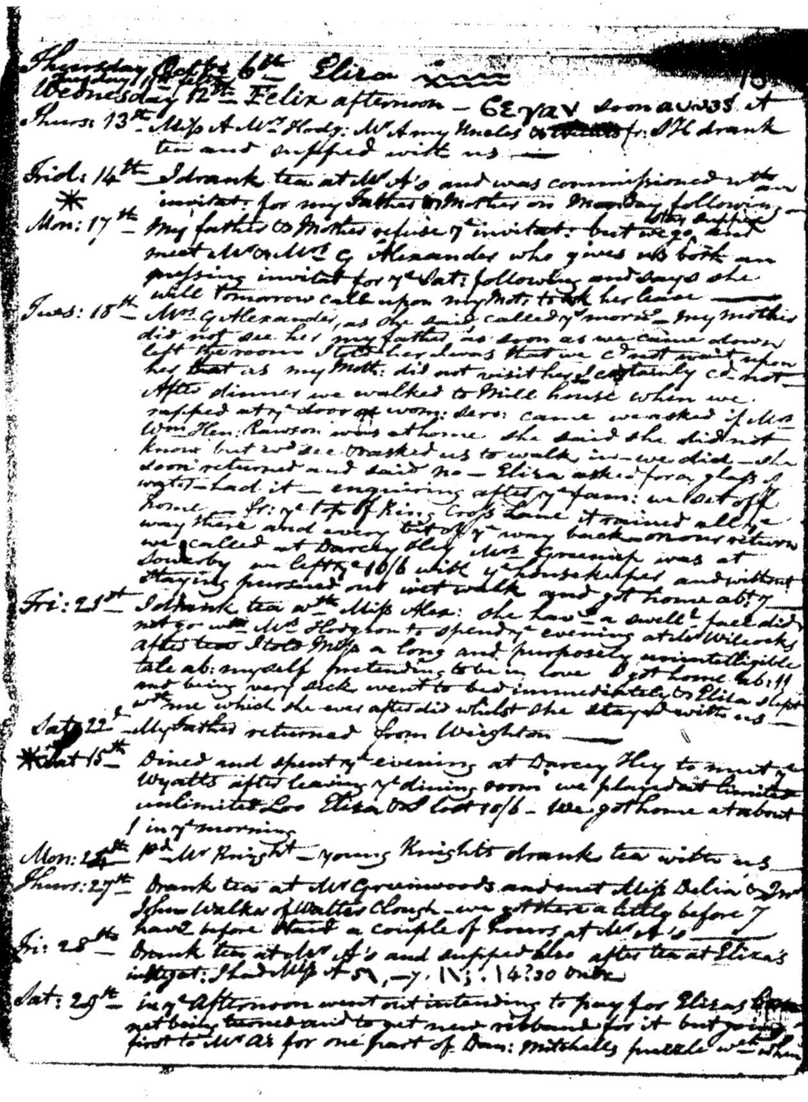

Thursday Oct[r] 6th Eliza [crypt]
Wednesday 12th Felix afternoon — [crypt]
Thurs: 13th Miss A & Mrs Hardy: Mr Amy Knoles [illegible] drank tea and supped with us —
Frid: 14th I drank tea at Mr A's and was commissioned with an invitat: for my Father & Mother on Monday following —
Mon: 17th My father & Mother refuse ye invitat: but we go, and meet Mr & Mrs G Alexander who gives us both an pressing invitat for ye Sat: following and says she will tomorrow call upon my Moth: to ask her leave —
Tues: 18th Mrs G Alexander, as she said called ye morn: my mother did not see her my father as soon as we came down left the room I told her [illegible] that we c[d] not wait upon her that as my Moth: did not visit her I certainly c[d] not — After dinner we walked to Mill house when we rapped at ye door a woman came we asked if Mrs Wm Hen: Rawson was at home she said she did not know but w[d] see & asked us to walk in — we did — she soon returned and said no — Eliza asked for a glass of water — had it — enquiring after ye farm: we set off home — fr: ye top of King Cross Lane it rained all ye way there and every bit of ye way back — on our return we called at Darcey Hey Mrs Greenup was at Sowerby we left ye 16/6 with ye housekeeper and without staying pursued our wet walk and got home ab[t] 7 —
Fri: 21st I drank tea with Miss Alex: she having a swell[d] face did not go with Mrs Hodgson to spend ye evening at old Wilcocks after tea I told Miss a long and purposely unintelligible tale ab: myself pretending to be in love I got home ab: 11 and being very sick went to bed immediately & Eliza slept wth me which she ever after did whilst she stayed with us —
Sat 22nd My father returned from Weighton —
*Sat 15th Dined and spent ye evening at Darcey Hey to meet ye Wyatts after leaving ye dining room we played at limited unlimited Loo Eliza & I lost 10/6 — We got home at about 1 in ye morning
Mon: 24th [illegible] Mr Knight — young Knights drank tea with us
Thurs: 27th Drank tea at Mr Greenwoods and met Miss Delia & Dr John Walker of Walters Clough — we got there a little before 7 have before stayed a couple of hours at Mr A's —
Fri: 28th Drank tea at Mr A's and supped also after tea at Eliza's [illegible]: I had Miss A [crypt]
Sat: 29th in ye afternoon went out intending to pay for Eliza's [illegible] not being turned and to get new ribband for it but going first to Mr A's for one part of Dun: Mitchell's puzzle with them

Anne Lister diary, 6-29 October 1808, SH:7/ML/E/26/1.

By kind permission of Alan Betteridge, Calderdale District Archives.

(Sadly Anne's diary petered out long before the death by drowning of Sam in 1813 [69] and before the lapsing in 1814 of her correspondence with Eliza, who was pronounced 'insane'.) We just get a sense of Anne's being increasingly taken up by her aunts and uncles; of her cosmopolitan York friends' growing more important to her; and of the tangle of rivalries between Anne, luckless Isabella, doomed Eliza, and Mariana Lawton whom Anne came to love.

Because of the haphazard way the Shibden papers were kept, this earliest diary, believed lost for so long, remains the least known. Thus none of the editors came very close to the young Anne Lister. John Lister, Phyllis Ramsden and Helena Whitbread did not have access to this volume. Muriel Green did look at it but claimed that 'from her diary, which begins at this period, it seems that her time was mainly occupied in study'.[70]

This earliest diary tells us less about Georgian England than the later volumes. But it is crucial for the *making* of Anne Lister. Read alongside the letters, it makes an important contribution to our understanding of pre-Victorian romantic friendship and lesbian sexuality. At this time, certain male homosexual acts could be punished by hanging; but in the eyes of the law, women - especially upper-middle-class women - were less likely to be touched by homosexual scandal. (An Edinburgh libel case brought in 1811 by two boarding-school mistresses accused of 'improper and criminal conduct' was in 1819 found by the House of Lords in their favour on the grounds that the 'crime here alleged has no existence'.)[71] It seems that the impeccable class credentials and girls' boarding-school respectability of Anne, Eliza and their friends allowed them considerable liberty - so long as they remained outwardly conventional and discreet.

Written in a sparse vigorous style, this earliest diary then is in many ways the most interesting, though hazardous to paginate and decipher. Anne Lister later reflected back on 'that feverish dream called youth': the feverish dream is brought to life here.[72]

Anne Lister in 1819

My second selected section, August to December 1819, covers about seven weeks and is about 18,500 words long, of which roughly a fifth is now in code.[73] Anne Lister was not only writing longer and more coded daily entries: she was also keeping her journal in a much more systematic way, with laborious indexing and cross-referencing. This evolution of a spontaneous diary into a more formal document reflected Anne's own dramatic change of class position. Since Sam's death Anne had increasingly distanced herself from her sister, mother and father (she now *'regretted his being so unlike a gentleman'*.)[74] As she had long hoped, she had made herself so amiable and indispensable to her Lister relations that in 1815 Anne finally left home to live with her elderly uncle James and his sister Anne at Shibden Hall, then an imposing but old-fashioned house set in a gentle valley and cut off from Halifax by a steep escarpment. (Her separation from her immediate family hardened with her mother's death in 1817).

With her position in the gentry now more assured, Anne continued her round of social visiting and gossip. She made a month's visit to Paris in May 1819 and her intellectual horizons continued to widen. Uncle James subscribed to a private Halifax library, and in the afternoons Anne browsed through its periodicals. There was a vogue then for chemistry and optics, for classifying minerals and soils, plants and animals: Anne absorbed it all and each day meticulously measured the temperature, air pressure and exact time of her readings. She had already started obsessively recording exactly how many hours she spent on each activity. Every single letter written or sermon heard was timed down to the exact minute. Sometimes she even combined walking and reading, climbing up the steep cobbled bank to Shibden, nose in her latest library book - perhaps a constitutional history of England or a new treatise on improving the postal service.[75] Her interest sprang partly from intense intellectual curiosity, partly from a practical need for up-to-date information. For if she was to inherit the Lister estate from Uncle James (Uncle Joseph had died in 1817) she needed to teach herself all she possibly could about estate management.

Anne Lister's 1819 entries reveal how her diaries had grown from their personal beginnings into detailed social documents shaped by wider developments, both locally and nationally. Much of day-to-day life in Halifax had changed little since her childhood: when visiting, Anne walked while her guest Isabella travelled on horseback behind William, a servant.[76] But meanwhile the town itself had grown since Anne's childhood: a contemporary *Commercial Directory* listed thirty 'merchants', twenty-four worsted manufacturers and eleven worsted spinners.[77] Nationally King George III had finally given way to the permanent Regency of his weak and disreputable son. Lord Liverpool and his Tory Cabinet tried to contain post-war economic and political troubles, assisted by a repressive legal system and by a network of country magistrates, local constables and - in times of crisis - special constables sworn in by the magistrates. The magistracy, relying on spies and informers, was in constant contact with the Home Office, so that troops could be allocated where tension was greatest. The struggle for reform in the face of repression culminated in the Peterloo Massacre of Monday 16 August 1819.

E. P. Thompson wrote his classic *The Making of the English Working Class* (1963) just a mile from Shibden. While his is history seen from below, Anne Lister's diary offers the reverse perspective - that the Halifax gentry, the special constables and the magistrate, all fearful in late 1819 of attacks on their property by the 'mob'. Thompson noted 'within two days of Peterloo, all England knew of the event. Within a week every detail of the massacre was being canvassed in alehouses, chapels, workshops, private houses.'[78] Anne Lister was among those who wanted up-to-the-minute news about what had happened and her diary tracks perceptions of events day by day. Even on Monday 16th itself, she noted 'Great many people about tonight in the streets - men talking together in groups of 15 or 20', and the next day wild rumours were flying:

> Everybody talking of the sad work at Manchester - a crowded meeting of these radical reformers . . . 500 women

"Dreadful Scene at Manchester: Meeting of Reformers, Aug. 16th 1819" (detail).
By kind permission of Manchester Public Libraries.

> in white with red caps of liberty . . . - the mob armed with pistols, & shot several people . . . But reports are so vague & monstrous, one scarce knows what to believe.[79]

Tales multiplied. On Wednesday, Anne heard that a Manchester constable 'who tore down the cap of liberty, [was] murdered by the mob', along with a Yeomanry Cavalry colonel. More alarming still, 'the reform infection seems to have reached us', with a 500-strong meeting 'among whom several women' on nearby Skircoat Moor. Anne had little doubt where her class interests lay:

> A man, dressed in black & on a black horse, was received with 3 cheers. He had given them some account of [the] Manchester meeting & was proceeding to other matter[s], when Mr Horton, a most active & spirited magistrate, made his appearance. The declaimer no sooner heard of this than he rode off, promising to be back in 40 minutes. Mr Hodgson however, the miller and constable, waited 50 minutes & the

> gentleman did not reappear. Mr H- remonstrated with them on their folly, saying . . . that if they did not disperse, he would read the riot act . . . On this they quietly dispersed. Whitley [bookseller and Anne's informant] has not been able to learn who was this dastardly fellow in black who no sooner got a scent of the magistracy than he left his deluded partizans in the lurch.[80]

The local regiment marched past, 'ordered off to Manchester', and Anne 'sat talking about these reform meetings' into the night with Isabella. On Thursday 'coaches brought word' from Manchester - that the colonel was *not* dead and indeed that the yeomanry had been drunk; Anne lamented that the regimental troops had not been called out instead, who 'would not have wanted liquor to give them courage'. Keen to keep abreast of events, she tracked down the one person in Halifax who took a Manchester newspaper. But interestingly, Anne Lister was not yet without some sympathy for the reformers. On Tuesday 24 August, she walked down to Halifax and happened to call:

> at a shoemaker to take shelter against a heavy shower. Detained 35 minutes. He was reading a last saturday's count[y] newspaper - thinks, as all the lower classes do, that the Manchester yeomanry well drunk & behaved very rashly & murder[ous]ly. Is for reform, but does not see what the reformers ha[ve] to do with caps of liberty, & flags, & bands of music at their meetings - a sensible, well-informed sort of man - astonished me by his knowledge of English history, but is evidently accustomed to read papers of an anti-ministerial turn - talks of taxation without representation & all the cant of the day.

(Eventually she reached her friends the Saltmarshes, a merchant family. Mr Saltmarshe, Anne learnt, 'and all the gentlemen in the town sworn in as special constables yesterday'.[81])

Protest continued that autumn including a mass meeting nearby on 4 October. Anne again followed it intently from a distance, noting

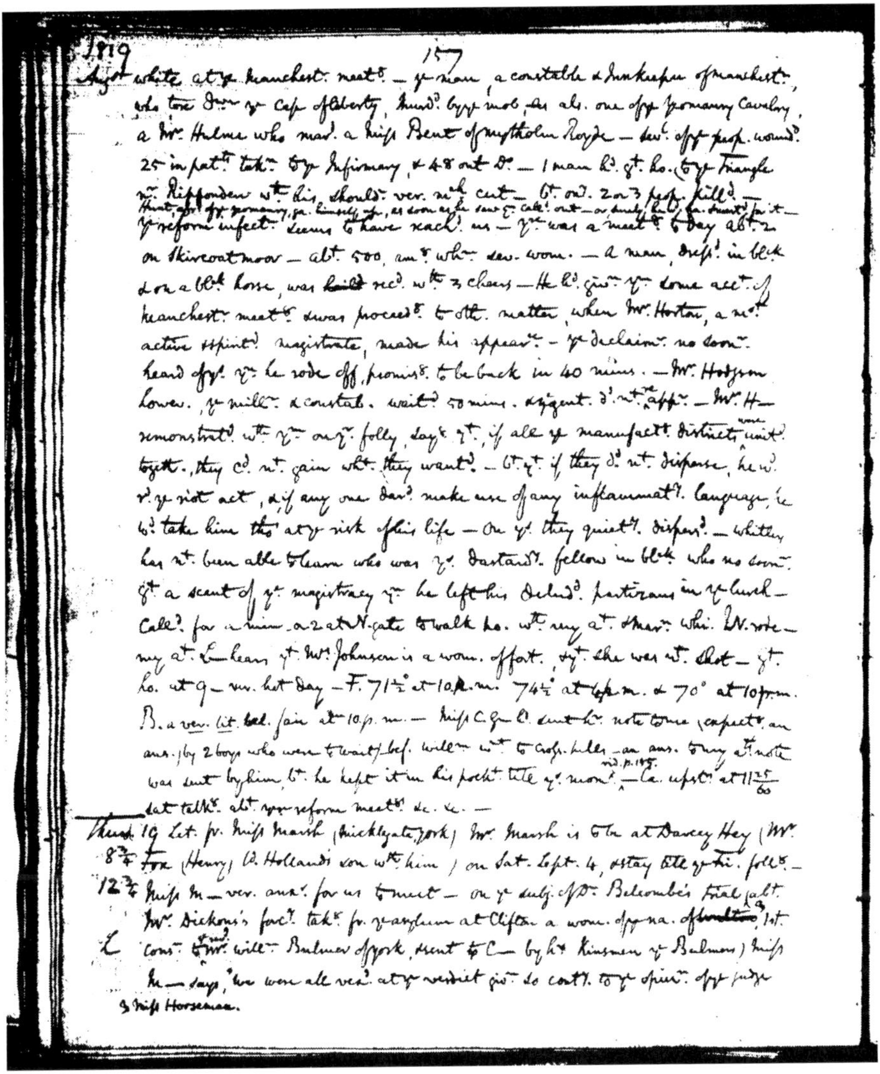
1819 157
Aug[t] white at ye Manchest[r]. meet[g]. – ye man, a constable & Innkeeper of Manchest[r], who tore down ye Cap of Liberty, murd[d]. by ye mob, as als. one of ye Yeomanry Cavalry, a Mr. Hulme who mar[d]. a Miss Bent of Mytholm Royde – sev[l]. of ye peop. wound[d]. 25 in pat[ts]. tak[n]. to ye Infirmary, & 48 out D[o]. – 1 man h[d]. g[t]. ho. (to ye Triangle nr. Ripponden wth his should[r]. ver. m[ch] cut – b[t]. on[l]. 2 or 3 peop. kill[d]. – [illegible] ye reform infect[n]. seems to have reach[d]. us – y[re] was a meet[g]. to day ab[t]. 2 on Skircoat moor – ab[t]. 500, am[g]. wh[m] sev. wom. – a man, dress[d]. in bl[ck] & on a bl[ck] horse, was ~~[illegible]~~ rec[d]. wth 3 cheers – He h[d]. giv[n]. y[m] some acc[t]. of Manchest[r]. meet[g]. & was proceed[g]. to oth. matter, when Mr. Horton, a m[ost] active & spirit[d]. magistrate, made his appear[ce]. – ye declaim[r]. no soon[r]. heard of y[t]. y[n]. he rode off, promis[g]. to be back in 40 mins. – Mr. Hodgson Lower, ye mill[r]. & constab. wait[d]. 50 mins. & ye gent. d[d]. n[t]. re-app[r]. – Mr. H– remonstrat[d]. wth y[m] on y[r]. folly, say[g]. y[t]. if all ye manufact[g]. districts were unit[d]. togeth., they c[d]. n[t]. gain wh[t]. they want[d]. – b[t]. y[t]. if they d[d]. n[t]. disperse, he w[d]. r[d]. ye riot act, & if any one dar[d]. make use of any inflammat[y]. language, he w[d]. take him tho' at ye risk of his life – On y[t]. they quiet[y]. dispers[d]. – Whitley has n[t]. been able to learn who was y[t]. dastard[y]. fellow in bl[ck]. who no soon[r]. g[t] a scent of y[e]. magistracy y[n]. he left his delud[d]. partizans in ye lurch – Call[d]. for a min. or 2 at N-gate to walk ho. wth my a[t]. & Mar[n]. Whi. W. wrote – my a[t]. & [illegible] hears y[t]. Mrs. Johnson is a wom. of fort. & y[t]. she was n[t]. shot – g[t]. ho. at 9 – ver. hot day – F. 71½° at 10 a.m. 74½° at 6 p.m. & 70° at 10 p.m. B. a ver. lit. bel. fair at 10 p.m. – Miss C. [illegible] sent h[r]. note to me, expect[g]. an ans. (by 2 boys who were to wait) bef. will[m] w[t]. to cross. hills – an ans. to my a[t]. note was sent by him, b[t]. he kept it in his pock[t]. till y[e]. morn[g]. (vid. p. 185.) – Ca. upst[s]. at 11 25/60 sat talk[g]. ab[t]. y[e] reform meet[g]. &c. &c. –
Thurs 19 Let. fr. Miss Marsh (Micklegate, York) Mr. Marsh is to be at Darcey Hey (Mr. Fox (Henry) D. Holland's son wth him) on Sat. Sept. 4, & stay till ye fri. foll[g]. –
8¾ Miss M– ver. anx[s]. for us to meet – on ye subj. of D[r]. Belcombe's trial (ab[t]. Mr. Dickons's forc[d]. tak[g]. fr. ye asylum at Clifton a wom. of ye na. of [illegible], 1st
12¾ cous[n]. to Mr. will[m]. Bulmer of York, & sent to C– by h[r] kinsmen ye Bulmers) Miss M– says, 'we were all vex[d]. at ye verdict giv[n]. so cont[y]. to ye opin[n]. of ye judge
L & Miss Horseman.

Anne Lister diary, 18-19 August 1819, SH:7/ML/E/3.
By kind permission of Calderdale District Archives.

disdainfully the 'sad shabby rag[ged] set'. A few days later when the Archbishop of York visited Halifax, 'a Radical (for these reformers do not like priests or bishops) [shouted] "A pig in a carriage, a pig in a carriage".'[82] Anne Lister may have been intrigued by female reformers and radical shoemakers; but staunch traditionalist and strict Anglican, her political allegiances were beginning to harden into the unshakeable Toryism of her later years.

*   *   *

Readers of *I Know My Own Heart* will recall that the diary for 1819 also records Anne Lister's continued quest for a woman with whom to share her life. But Isabella Norcliffe's visit confirmed her in Anne's eyes as coarse and indiscreet: '*her habits are very little suited to mine. I could not live happily with her. At all events the experiment shall not be tried*'.[83] Mariana Lawton, though much less accessible since her marriage, remained Anne's main love; and, as Whitbread's edition records, Anne had now begun a flirtation with pretty Miss Brown. But although her father, Copley Brown, was a loyal opponent of reform, he had made money from his cardmaking business and the Listers did not consort with 'tradesmen' - and the doomed relationship petered out with Miss Brown's marriage.

Anne Lister's use of her secret code, now comprising perhaps a fifth of her diary, had settled into a routine. She used code to confide her personal anxieties: about a distant Lister relative who might inherit Shibden; her humiliation at her own lack of independent income *('mending my black silk legs till near twelve')* and her embarrassment at Isabella's indiscretions. But the longest coded passages record her stratagems for winning Miss Brown, other flirtations and her sexual relations with Isabella (who '*was for going to sleep, but I would have a kiss. She says it gives her a pain in her back*').[84] The intimate coded passages now form a minor though important key running through the diary, counterpointing the major key of the more public face of Anne Lister.

What did successive editors select from late 1819? John Lister's edition is full of intriguing social detail, but omits the Peterloo passages, not picking up the story of 'the Reform agitation' until late

October (and noting unsympathetically that 'the West Riding was then notorious as being a seat of disaffection and discontent').[85] Ramsden offers a summary of the 'crypt passages' for these months but this is too bland to help much.[86] Luckily, readers can now turn to *I Know My Own Heart* to trace Anne's desolation over Mariana, Isabella's troubled visit and the courtship of Miss Brown. But Whitbread, like John Lister, does not pick up on Peterloo until mid-November and Anne's visit to Manchester, making it hard for students to place Peterloo and local reform meetings in context.[87]

What then is the value to the historian of the diary here? Read alongside other contemporary accounts, it allows us to build up a day-by-day picture of how the upper middle class in one Yorkshire manufacturing town responded to the drama of Peterloo. Second, it offers what is probably a uniquely candid account of the boundaries - outward respectability and considerable discretion - within which lesbian relationships among the elite might be enjoyed. As a result, this section holds the reader's attention closely.[88]

Anne Lister in 1832

My third selection combines the courtship of Ann Walker and the first election after the 1832 Reform Act. Covering about five weeks in autumn 1832, it comprises about 20,000 words of which still roughly a fifth is in code. However the pace of the diary has slowed further and Anne's handwriting is less easy to read.[89]

Anne Lister's life had again changed dramatically since 1819. Uncle James died in 1826; his will unambiguously made her sole executrix and bequeathed the whole estate to her - provided she allowed her father and aunt to receive rents from the tenancies and profits from his canal shares.[90] By 1832, therefore, forty-one-year-old Anne was living at Shibden with her elderly father and aunt, sister Marian and servants. Her aunt seemed to run the household (domestic detail still scarcely surfaced in the diary) while Anne ran the estate with the help of a steward. This meant that Anne, although not yet in full possession of the estate, had at last considerable financial independence. She travelled to Switzerland and Italy, the Pyrenees and Rhine, and even lived periodically in Paris, studying science, enjoying embassy society and making the aristocratic friendships that she had so long coveted.[91] More cosmopolitan and confident, Anne returned to Shibden in May 1832. Uncle James's will combined with her talent for strategic friendships now established her as a respectable if unusual member of the landed gentry.

She came home to a Halifax expanding fast. An 1828 extension brought the canal right up to the town centre, and new road engineering also made local travel easier. The township population had grown from 11,000 to 20,000 in thirty years (although already outstripped by nearby Bradford). Steam power, used in Lancashire's cotton factories, could now bc adapted to West Riding worsted mills. The Factory Inquiry Commission (1834) into child labour revealed how a newer generation of manufacturers had begun to dwarf the old. The Listers' friends the Rawsons and Saltmarshes still had a woollen cloth-dressing mill, now steam-powered, which employed eighty-one people. But the large factories, with up to 550 employees, were the newly-built steam-powered spinning mills of industrialists like James Akroyd and John Holdsworth. Anne, unimpressed by this new money, lamented that 'the affairs of the town are now quite in the hands of second-rate people'.[92]

Perched above Halifax in Shibden Hall, she was well placed to observe this industrialization but largely kept her distance from the textile industry. Like other members of the gentry, she was much more involved in extractive and transport industries than in manufacturing - in selling or leasing at the highest price obtainable land for building, stone for road-making and coal for steam engines. Through her solicitor or steward she haggled keenly over prices and leases. With her rentals from tenants, this just allowed Anne Lister to maintain the Shibden household, to travel extensively and to improve the estate. Indeed, much of the diary for late 1832 is crammed with detail of how Anne supervised the men employed to move soil and plant trees. She had an elegant walk with a rustic seat and thatched garden hut built; the library improved; and a new footman taken on. ('No objection to give £20 wages if that is to include washing . . . -

his being able to read and write, indispensable'.) For Anne's new sophisticated friends increased her dissatisfaction with the house she had inherited: she longed for it to be grand and imposing. But her aristocratic ambitions already outstripped her modest estate income. She confessed to her diary that she 'must go & live on bread and water - whether I shall do so or not is doubtful'.[93]

Another call upon her purse was the cost of supporting the Tories at elections. When Anne returned to Shibden in mid-1832, the Whig Reform Bill was about to receive the Royal Assent. From Paris, Anne had followed the reform agitation with keen interest.[94] She showed less interest in the new exclusion from the parliamentary franchise of propertied women like herself than in Halifax's gaining not just one but two MPs of its own. Here the Lister diaries offer wonderful source material for understanding the ways in which 1832 signalled electoral change - new middle-class voters, new urban constituencies, an exclusively male franchise - and how much, with no secret ballot yet, it merely perpetuated landowner dominance. Indeed Anne Lister, who perhaps had around twenty enfranchised male tenants to bully, arguably had far more political power as a landowner than any individual voter.[95] And she could exercise this influence very effectively in the new compact Halifax borough constituency. (This despite the fact Shibden Hall itself lay in the rural West Riding county constituency: here the Listers were but political minnows compared to such great landowners as Earl Fitzwilliam and Lord Wharncliffe who could exert enormous 'influence' respectively for the Whigs and the Tories.)

As readers of the John Lister and Muriel Green editions know, in the December 1832 election Anne Lister had no hesitation in loyally supporting Halifax's Tory candidate, the Honourable James Stuart Wortley. He was standing against two Whig-Liberal candidates and a Whig-Radical. Anne set to work:

> Note from Mr Parker from Mr Wortley's committee room begging me to make sure of John Bottomley's vote . . . Had John Bottomley, having sent for him to tell him to vote for Wortley tomorrow - had 1/4 hour's talk - he promised to vote for him tomorrow or thursday as he had a job he must do

> tomorrow - they [Whigs?] had all been at him, & some said they would not employ him again if he would not vote their way - but he told them how I wanted him to vote, and seeming to care nothing about it but that he thought he ought to oblige me. It is quite useless to leave such men as he uninfluenced. He knows nothing & cares nothing about it, & is li[kel]y best satisfied with the idea of pleasing somebody he knows.[96]

A farmer, John Bottomley is listed in the 1832 *Register of the Electors to Vote* and the subsequent *Poll Book* records how he dutifully cast a 'plumper' for Wortley.[97] Despite such helpful arm-twisting by Tory landowners like Anne living just outside the constituency and despite her contributions to Tory election expenses, Wortley lost. 'The spirit of Radicalism is fearfully strong', Anne lamented afterwards; 'the dissenters are so united against us, I do not see how we can make head against them'.[98]

* * *

Anne Lister's 1832 diary also shows her continuing to read widely, including Plutarch's *Lives,* a history of modern Greece and - to help her estate improvement - a forester's guide. She also maintained a vigorous correspondence with both new friends and old - like Mariana Lawton and Isabella Norcliffe. In December she philosophically reviewed her life in a letter to Mariana:

> The thought of exile from poor Shibden always makes me melancholy. Come what may, I have been happier here than anywhere else . . . Providence ordains all things wisely - I am perfectly contented . . . I am attached to my own people - they are accustomed to my oddities, are kind, are civilized to me . . . But . . . a great deal will, & must, depend on that someone known or unknown, whom I still hope for as the comfort of my evening hour.[99]

This was disingenuous: Anne had already met 'that someone', Ann

Walker, living alone at Lidgate in Lightcliffe, about two miles away. Anne Lister's candid account of her calculating courtship of this shy young heiress occupies most of the coded passages for late 1832, yet remains a little known sections of the diary.

September 1832 opened on Anne's lonely discontents: her relationship with Mariana was unsatisfactory and her income was insufficient for living in the style she desired. Friendship with wealthy Ann Walker was a godsend. What could be more natural for these two respectable neighbours to pay a formal round of calls together in Ann Walker's carriage? (Anne Lister, still keen to hide signs of shabbiness, confided in her diary *'sewing watch pocket in new pelisse & putting strings to petticoat & getting all ready to put on tomorrow to go with Miss Walker'*.) They called upon the houses of the gentry, upon Mrs Saltmarshe and others, leaving cards 'then made sundry shoppings & Miss W- set me down at our own gate at 5 1/2'. Anne Lister hastily changed her clothes, going out to supervise the men working on 'the walk' - but later that day noted that '*Miss W & I got on very well . . . If she was fond of me & manageable, I think I could be comfortable enough with her.*' They chose shrubs for each other, exchanged books and discussed plans for spending Easter in Rome. Anne, whose diary entries now often began erotically with *'incurred a cross last night thinking of Miss Walker'*, determined on seduction.[100] They met at Lidgate then walking slowly back, 'sauntered . . . in my walk - then on returning rested in the hut & must have sat there a couple of hours', an unusually vague bit of time-keeping for Anne; but as she confessed in code later that day:

> *Miss W- & I very cozy & confidential . . . She sat in the moss house hardly liking to move - of course I made myself agreeable & I think she already likes me even more than she herself is aware.. She seems to take all I say for gospel . . . She said she would call on my aunt on Monday . . . I really did feel rather in love with her in the hut & as we returned. I shall pay due court for the next few months, & after all I really think I can make her happy & myself too . . . We laughed at the idea of the talk our going abroad together would [produce]. She said it would be as good as a*

marriage. 'Yes', said [I], 'quite as good or better'. She falls into my view of things admirably . . . We shall have money enough. She will look up to me & soon feel attached & I, after all my moils [turmoils], shall be steady, &, if God so wills it, happy . . . I can gently mould Miss W to my wishes; & may we not be happy? How strange the fate [of] things! If after all, my companion for life should be Miss Walker. She was nine & twenty a little while ago! How little my aunt or anyone suspects what I am about! [101]

The following day Ann Walker did indeed pay a formal visit to Shibden. Afterwards the two women sat in the hut for three-quarters of an hour. Anne Lister later confided in her diary

Bordering on love-making in the hut . . . Our liaison is now established . . . I am reprovided [for] & the object of my choice have perhaps three thousand a year or near it - probably two-thirds at her own disposal.[102]

The nature of Anne Lister's seducing a lifelong companion became clear: romantic and sexual, financial and instrumental. She accepted as natural and God-given the Christian morality of so respectable and discreet a relationship. But Ann Walker's moody vacillations about going abroad began to irk her. There was coolness and distrust, tears then reconciliation. For Anne Lister however the attraction of travelling in style with English and French servants was too great to forgo:

Talked to Miss W- of going to York . . . To take plate & linen & have a good handsome lodging, & to call James by his sirname [sic], & make him powder, & have Joseph Booth under him - Sarah to be cook-housekeeper & Eugenie to meet us. A very nice plan as she seemed to think. I laughed & said, 'Well, & after that, Leamington & then the south.' 'Yes', said she, '& then you mean abroad. But I will not go' - and then she got into the old story of [how] she felt she was not doing right morally, could not consent, had determined to

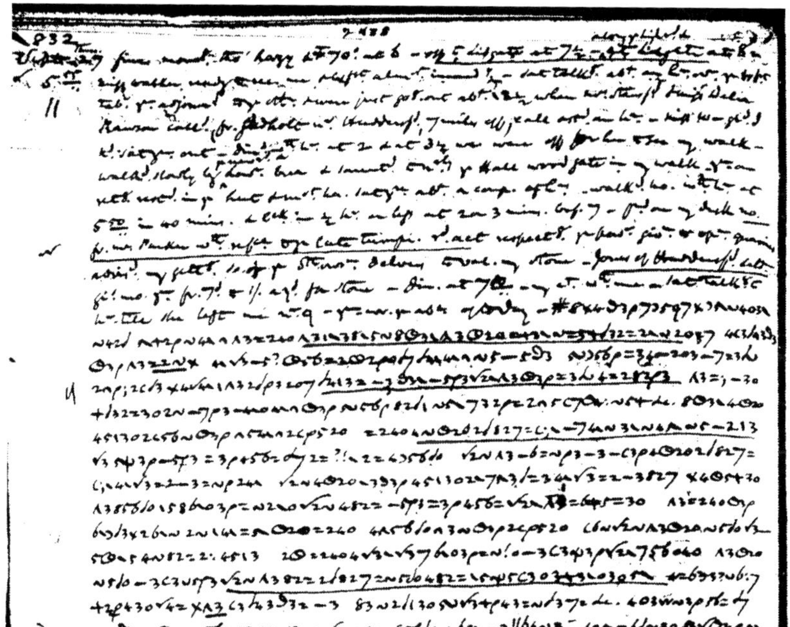

Anne Lister diary, 27 September 1832, SH:7/ML/E/15.

By kind permission of Calderdale District Archives.

say no. I laughed it all off at the moment. She grieved over behaving so ill on Wednesday night - . . . yet let me grubble [grope] her this morning gladly enough.[103]

Ann Walker's equivocation continued. Anne Lister spent the night at Lidgate, trying to use their love-making to sanctify the relationship more formally, hinting *'that our present intercourse without any tie between us must be as wrong as any other transient connection'*. Later that day,

Miss W- told me in the hut if she said 'yes' again it should be binding. It should be the same as a marriage & she would give me no cause to be jealous. [She] made no objection to what I proposed, that is, her de[c]laring it on the Bible & taking the sa[c]rament with me at Shibden or Lightcliffe church.[104]

Some contemporary readers, aware that Anne rejected heterosexuality, may find puzzling such references to church ritual and to lesbian marriage (including all the property implications that marriage then had). Similarly some may be startled by Anne's detailed recording of the seemingly abrupt switching between male and female gender roles, pleasure and business, grubbling and haggling.[105]

This section of the diary therefore offered particular challenge to successive editors. Both John Lister and Muriel Green present all the rich social and political detail, but introduce only cursorily the Ann Walker relationship; while Phyllis Ramsden's valuable summary of the coded passages is also unhelpfully euphemistic.[106]

The diary for this period, then, is of particular interest to historians - both in its political information and in the unrestrained detail of the coded sections, possibly unequalled in lesbianism historiography. However, some of the barrowing, channelling and culverting details are tedious to all but a landscape historian collecting data; and Anne Lister's complete obsession with recording time can irritate. A firm editorial hand would need to excise mundane repetition from a transcript, leaving in sharper focus the apparent tensions in Anne Lister's life - between desire to share her life with another woman yet desire for outwardly conventional respectability: between wanting to exploit new industrial opportunities yet resentment that the influence of minor landed gentry like the Listers was being challenged by the rising Whig manufacturers like Akroyd. 'The quiet days of old have parted never to return', she wrote, sensing that perhaps her time too was passing.[107] Eventually Anne Lister persuaded the melancholy Ann Walker to live with her at Shibden; but Chartist disturbances were now added to her money worries. They decided to leave Britain to travel to Russia and reached Moscow in October 1839.

Anne Lister, Her Diaries and the Historians

This historiographical assessment, necessarily provisional given the wealth of archive material, prompts more questions. For historians will rightly be impatient to know, after all the cautionary hedging about, where lies the major contribution of Anne Lister and of her journals to early nineteenth-century English history.

What was Anne's objective class position? Born into an ill-starred branch of an ancient landowning family, she developed inheritance ambitions, slipped into the minor gentry, and then socially - if not financially - entered aristocratic circles in the 1830s as a European (and particularly Russian) traveller. This upward social mobility, accelerated by her genius for cultivating advantageous friendships, allowed Anne to enjoy considerable licence. But within this class, how unusual was it for a woman to inherit an estate over a more distant male heir?[108] We know other women owned and ran estates; but how many of them were widows, rather than women like Anne who had rejected conventional marriage? Was there anything distinctive in Anne Lister's entrepreneurial energy or did it fit the usual gentry response to industrial opportunities?[109] Finally, we know wealthy women wielded considerable political influence; yet how usual among women with smaller-scale estates was Anne's direct exertion of economic power? For instance, how many other female landowners might attend a crucial meeting of local canal shareholders threatened by the coming railways and, the only woman present, make their arguments heard?[110]

Like wealthy wives who, having provided their husbands with 'an heir and spare', could then indulge in other affairs, Anne enjoyed far more liberties than the middle-class women whom she so disdained.[111] But did many of her contemporaries also reject taking a husband, preferring to find female partners? Put another way, how extensive *was* Anne's lesbian network, and to what extent were she and her friends part of a culture which, so long as discretion was maintained, could enjoy considerable licence?[112] It is clear from Eliza's calling Anne 'my husband' to her later domination of Ann Walker, that Anne opted for a masculine role; did this entail more risks compared to her gender-conforming partners? Finally, as Chartism loomed towards the end of her life, Anne seemed to sense her world was passing. Some editors suggested she was 'far in advance of her time'; but does not Anne's very language - archaicisms like 'grubble' - reveal her as more *pre*-Victorian?[113] Would the next generation of women be able to enjoy such a full range of liberties?

The diaries raise as many questions as their writer. *Why* did she write them so obsessively and at such length? How much was it pride in her own achievements, how much was the very act of laboriously writing down each encounter in such detail a way to withstand frustations and setbacks?[114] Which other early nineteenth-century English diaries offer such a fascinating mixture of old and new - leeches and railways - and range so widely in their subject matter? Anne Lister's recording of one woman's political and entrepreneurial, intellectual and sexual activities makes these diaries incomprably rich source material. Women of Anne's generation had access neither to the university education nor to the public preferment of, say, Samuel Pepys or James Boswell; but her days are crammed with a magical mix of the public and private spheres, and the journals record it all.

The long suppression of the coded passages, followed by Whitbread's 1988 edition, prompted energetic debate. Some still claim Anne's lesbianism is irrelevant to any serious assessment of the journals; others, aware of the diaries' invaluable contribution to lesbian historiography,[115] argue that the intimate coded sections outshine all the rest and may even be enjoyed on their own. Anne Lister was a controversial figure during her lifetime: she remains so two centuries later, and the debate continues.[116]

Here I have suggested that lesbianism is a crucial theme but not the only theme; and have argued the importance of seeing the diaries as a *whole* in order to reflect the overall *balance* of Anne Lister's life. But the four-million words continues to present tremendous methodological problems. In order not to 'retreat, thoroughly demoralised and half-blind', researchers keen to work on this magnificent material need to make clear choices about criteria for omission and selection, and need to be open about those choices [117] and about their debts to previous editors, so that the long-awaited critical reassessment can gradually take shape.

Anne Lister of Shibden Hall

Re-reading the Correspondence

The four-million word diaries, the jewel in the Anne Lister crown, have long attracted editors. In the late nineteenth century John Lister published his selections and cracked the code in which about a sixth of the journals are written; later Phyllis Ramsden summarised the diaries' coded passages and worked on Anne's travel writings; then in the 1980s a project at Birmingham University transcribed about 15% of the journals; and most recently Helena Whitbread's two published selections offered to national readership the private world of Anne's lesbian relationships previously buried in the code.[1] Of these successive editors, Muriel Green alone has given primary focus to the letters.[2] Her selection from the vast Anne Lister correspondence, *Miss Lister of Shibden Hall: Selected Letters (1800-1840)* published in 1992, probably represents something of a record.[3] Her patient and dedicated hard work was begun no less than sixty years ago - in 1933. But it has at last paid off: her book stands alone and will be welcomed by antiquarians and general readers alike.

Miss Lister of Shibden Hall offers a succinct and accessible guide to the broad outline of Anne's extraordinary life. While Whitbread's selections provide a detailed and intimate narrative for the years

1817-24 and 1824-26, Green's slimmer book allows us to follow Anne's life over a period of forty years in the space of some 200 pages (a fast gallop of just five pages per year).[4] The eighty nine letters selected begin with nine-year-old Anne's first letter, written in 1800 in Ripon to her favourite Lister aunt, Anne at Shibden Hall, politely sending 'my Duty to my Uncles and Aunts' and explaining 'I like Music better then [sic] Dancing and am very happy at School'. It then leads the reader briskly by way of letters written from Shibden, Anne's home after 1815, and others from Paris describing successive visits from 1819 onwards - plus her more adventurous travels in the 1830s to the Pyrenees, Denmark and Switzerland. Green's book then finally moves on to Anne Lister's most ambitious - and, it turned out, fatal - journey through Russia to Moscow, then southwards towards the Caucasus Mountains, and so on to the last letter in this volume, dated May 1840, describing 'galloping across the frozen Volga' and her visit to Kazan. 'This fine old Tatar capital did not disappoint us... We had a Tatar breakfast, and were admitted into a Tatar haram, and attended divine service in the great mosque.'[5]

Green's edition confirms Anne Lister's remarkable talents: her skill in building and sustaining close relationships with an increasingly sophisticated range of women correspondents; her ability in running the Shibden estate, which she eventually inherited; and - most especially - her intrepid zest for European travel. In all this, *Miss Lister of Shibden Hall* represents a brave achievement.

But such a compact anthology necessarily prompts questions. How were the eighty-nine letters chosen and how many have been left out? Are there themes which have been omitted? How representative is the selection presented here? Readers intrigued by such questions will want to turn to Green's much earlier dissertation, completed in 1938, representing a more substantial transcription of the correspondence and entitled *A Spirited Yorkshirewoman: the Letters of Anne Lister of Shibden Hall, Halifax b 1791 - d 1840.*[6] For publication of Green's book offers a timely opportunity to review the correspondence and to compare its value to Anne Lister scholars with that of the journals.

Muriel Green enters Shibden Hall

After Anne Lister's death in 1840, her companion Ann Walker returned to Shibden Hall. The estate became subject to protracted inheritance disputes.[7] Eventually, in 1855 it was duly claimed by a very distant branch of the Lister family - the great-grandson of Thomas of Virginia (1708-40), brother of Jeremy Lister who was Anne's grandfather.[8] Young John Lister, only eight years old when his family finally occupied Shibden Hall, became the first scholar to work seriously on the voluminous Anne Lister manuscripts. Between 1887 and 1892 the *Halifax Guardian* published his selections from her diaries. From 1900, as first president of the Halifax Antiquarian Society, he continued to publish regularly his local history research in the Society's *Transactions*. Although distressed by the portrait of Anne Lister revealed in the passages in the code he had cracked, he decided not to burn the volumes. But he published no more about her.[9]

When John Lister died in October 1933 Shibden became the property of Halifax borough, and so the vast jumble of family papers fell to the local council.[10] The borough librarian, Edward Green, received permission to enter the Hall. With him went his young daughter Muriel, also on the library staff and the person now with the job of bringing order to chaos. The visit made a vivid impression on her:

> At first the little study at Shibden Hall had a most discouraging appearance. The books overflowed from the shelves on to the chairs and tables and even on to the floor. There were numerous large and dusty trunks containing leases, wills, accounts, recipes, funeral notes, diaries, letters, etc. and from time to time another trunk or box of MSS. would turn up from beneath a pile of lumber from some other part of the house.[11]

Her first task was to catalogue John Lister's extensive collection of books and this alone took two years.[12] Muriel Green then turned her attention to the innumerable Lister letters. She divided them into ten broad categories, so that those of 'the most important people are kept together', and then systematically wrote a catalogue card for each item, giving the date as accurately as possible along with a brief summary of the contents.[13]

One category was, of course, the Anne Lister correspondence; fascinated, Muriel Green took the main letters home to transcribe them so she could base her Library Association dissertation upon them. She dipped into the diaries to check points in the correspondence but otherwise concentrated on the letters.[14] From this painstaking work, in 1936 Green published in the *Halifax Courier and Guardian* a series of twelve articles, 'A Woman in Advance of Her Times: The Letters of Anne Lister of Shibden Hall';[15] and produced her professional librarian's listing of 'The Shibden Hall Muniments' two years later.[16] Also in 1938 she completed her dissertation, *A Spirited Yorkshirewoman,* representing a 250,000-word transcription of no fewer than 395 letters - more than four times as many as in her book half-a-century later.[17]

A librarian's portrait, the dissertation is systematic, thorough and is usefully indexed, but contains little editorial matter. However, it does begin to provide answers to some of the questions prompted by Muriel Green's own much shorter 1992 anthology. There are obvious similarities between both the dissertation and the book - in particular, the strong (and overlapping) focus on letters written to aunt Anne, on European travel and on descriptions of life in Paris.

But other themes strongly represented in the dissertation have been cut down for the book. The nine letters between Anne and her only surviving (and much loved) brother, Samuel, when he was away in the army, have been reduced to one; so readers miss the revealing insights from, for instance, an 1811 letter in which twenty-year-old Anne chafes over girls' restricted freedoms then:

> My high opinion of you, my dear Sam is as unbounded as my affection for you . . . Never till this moment did I feel a wish to be freed from that petticoat slavery that but ill subdues a mind superior to its tyranny . . . Sometimes I could envy you,

if it were not impious and unjust . . . Of myself I have little to say. Doomed perhaps to be a fixture through life, few circumstances are likely to occur to me worthy [of] much attention . . .[18]

Similarly, over a dozen letters in the dissertation chapter 'Eliza Raine's Letters 1806-1814' have been reduced in the intervening half- century to just one short letter addressed to 'My dearest Eliza' - which fails to illuminate the full significance of this intensely intimate schoolgirl relationship. Likewise, the dissertation chapter entitled 'One Friend to Another 1810', comprising a dozen long letters between Anne and her friend Isabella Norcliffe of Langton Hall in the East Riding, has been excised completely from the book. Yet a glance at the formal rhetorical flourishes in these dozen letters again suggests a significant and complex relationship. For instance, in 1810 Anne wrote:

Since my dearest Isabella there is nothing which can give me [more] pleasure on the day when I leave my kind and much loved friends at Red house [in York] but seeing you I cannot but flatter myself with the hope that this last remaining consolation will not be denied me by any engagement on your part . . . I trust my dear Isabella the nature of this specimen of my handwriting may be such that you cannot in conscience doom me to the stillness of your silence eloquent. If heaven taught letters for some wretch's aid a banish'd lover or a captive maid, would that I were either of these that I might have some better claim to that valuable aid to my pleasure which the pen of Isabella can only give to the heart of that one who is less sincerely than happily her firmly and tenderly attached friend A. Lister.[19]

Those reading only Green's 1992 book and not the 1938 dissertation would therefore miss much of the subtle but crucial shifts in style over a matter of years, from the perky artlessness of her childhood letters to this mannered rhetoric. Clearly Anne had developed the skill to use her own scholarly cleverness to manipulate selected female correspondents.[20] Readers would regret that so much of the richness of the dissertation had to be cut for the book. Indeed, those now aware of Anne Lister's lesbianism, will be particularly puzzled by the cautious and traditional portrait still presented by Muriel Green in 1992.[21]

So eventually Anne Lister scholars will find that Green's dissertation has so whetted their appetite that they must go back to read the original manuscript letters themselves. Remarkably, approximately 1,850 - about five times the number in the dissertation - Anne Lister letters have been preserved, in Calderdale District Archives.[22] So, guided by Muriel Green's invaluable 1930s signposting, the remainder of this article moves into the Archives in Halifax Library to investigate the original correspondence.

Into the Archives

Drawing closely upon Green's pioneering 1938 catalogue, a revised 'Shibden Hall Muniments' listing evolved and the new list, produced in 1983, expands the Anne Lister entry. The original ten sub-divisions within the 'Lister Letters' category are now organised into twenty-three, of which no fewer than twelve cover the Anne Lister material. These twelve sub-divisions contain a large general correspondence category; plus smaller groupings of specific letters (such as those between Anne and Eliza Raine, and Anne's business letters); the twenty-seven volumes of her journals; plus account books and miscellaneous notes.[23]

This new list leads the researcher entering Calderdale Archives to two small compact drawers of neat catalogue cards;[24] these point to twenty-seven stout containers of Anne Lister's manuscript material kept in the strongroom in Halifax Library. Guided by the archivist, the researcher can begin to look inside the boxes and read the letters in the original hand, just as they were written.

Of the 1,850 Anne Lister letters which survive[25] about half are letters are *from* Anne Lister; the rest are mainly *to* Anne Lister (or are documents other than letters, or are letters both *to* and from correspondents other than Anne herself). Of these, those letters *from* Anne Lister are probably of particular interest, because - like the diaries - they allow the reader to come as close as possible to Anne herself, hearing her own voice distinctly in conversation with her friends. But of these nine hundred letters from Anne Lister, about 710 are either drafts or copies, and only about 190 are the original manuscript letters as Anne herself actually wrote them - and which she then posted (or sent by servant or messenger).[26]

So although only about 10% of the total number of letters are originals from Anne, these immediately prompt intriguing speculation. How did these 190 letters *from* Anne find their way back into the Shibden Hall collection? For the great majority, the reason is obvious: they were mainly written to Aunt Anne, (or to Anne Lister's mother, brother Samuel, uncle James, sister Marian or other family members). The Shibden Hall Muniments is the obvious repository for such family correspondence.[27] Of the remaining two dozen original letters, most were written to Anne Lister's well-connected Scottish friend, Sibbella MacLean; and the others to Isabella Norcliffe. If Anne had actually asked these two close women friends to return her own letters, this may suggest the great significance of such personal correspondence to her, and perhaps her fear they should fall into unsympathetic hands.

Equally intriguing is that more than seven hundred letters *from* Anne are preserved among the Shibden Hall papers in either a copy or in draft form. Over 500 of these have immediate explanation in that they are drafts or copies of business letters.[28]After her uncle James died in January 1826, Anne took over the major responsibility for running the Shibden estate; and from the deaths of her father and aunt in 1836, she became solely responsible for this complex enterprise. Three notebooks, covering the period July 1826 to May 1838, survive and are crammed with meticulous drafts of business letters, eloquent testimony to Anne Lister's brisk commercial acumen. One brief example from this matter-of- fact correspondence, selected almost at random, illustrates how competently she ran the Shibden estate:

Mrs Lister sends Mr Parker the Walsh-land conveyance-bond & Receipt, and will be glad to hear whether he is able to make any satisfactory arrangement respecting the purchaser of a line of ground . . .
Shibden Hall
Sunday evening 13 November 1836
Messrs Parker & Adam}
Solicitors }
Halifax }

enclosed in a sealed parcel containing the 2 above named papers & sent by Frank tonight. [29]

The remaining drafts and copies are more intriguing, because they comprise mainly letters Anne wrote to female friends. These women were either minor but well-placed members of the aristocracy - Lady Stuart, Lady Stuart de Rothesay, Lady Gordon - whose good opinion she dearly needed to cultivate; or women with whom she had a lesbian relationship - Maria Barlow in Paris, Mariana Lawton in Cheshire, and Ann Walker, the wealthy neighbour who came to live with Anne Lister at Shibden Hall in 1834. The preservation of drafts and copies of such purely personal letters clearly suggests who among her many correspondents had a particular significance for Anne Lister: for them she had to get the letter *right* . They confirm the extraordinary importance letters then played in the complex web of female friendships - and let us glimpse what was especially important to Anne Lister: upward social and economic mobility plus sexuality.[30] Where these two key elements in Anne's character combine, the letters need to be re-read alongside other documents. In 1833, for instance, just a few months after the start of her determined courtship of Ann Walker, Anne Lister wrote from Shibden to her young neighbour, then visiting in Scotland, about her own travel plans - and wrote a rough draft of this letter first:

As I have no longer the same interest here I had some months ago, I am more and more impatient to be off . . . I am in the midst of looking over books, papers etc preparatory to leaving home for some time; for, if my aunt and father continue well, I feel no inclination to hurry back . . .[31]

On the face of it, a very matter-of-fact note. So why the draft? Phyllis Ramsden's summaries of the coded passages of the diary ('AW regretting promise to "marry" AL etc'.) suggests one reading of the letter: Anne Lister was using her own travel plans to manipulate Ann Walker's feeling towards her.[32] In another example, from June 1835, Anne Lister wrote a draft of a letter to Ann Walker's brother-in-law; the letter was to go under Ann Walker's signature and concerned the controversial 'division of the estate': Anne Lister suggested that Ann Walker should maintain 'I have still the same reasons that I had for being anxious to expedite the conclusion of the business as much as possible; and I hope the papers will be ready for signing before the end of next month', courtesy of Messrs Gray, the York solicitors.[33] Such illuminating drafts of correspondence, read alongside Anne Lister coded financial jottings for 1835 *('A's rents per annum 407.12.6 . . . Lot one if she gets it 1527.7.3')* suggests how extraordinarily keen were Anne Lister's financial ambitions concerning her developing intimacy with Ann Walker.[34]

* * *

Beyond this, it is more difficult to group the correspondence by subject or theme because inevitably Anne Lister's letters about travel spill over into news about friends, a letter about her aunt's health merges into gossip about local politics or some problem on the estate. But it is useful to compare the weight given in Muriel Green's book to Anne's correspondence with aunt Anne about travel against that in the original letters: about half the letters in the book are from Anne to her aunt, mainly about Anne's travels; but in the original correspondence only about 7% are to her aunt (again mainly about travel).

This is a considerable discrepancy. Partly it is explained by the large number of business letters in the collection which in the 1930s Muriel Green understandably only had time to catalogue together as three notebooks, and so business correspondence is heavily under-represented in her dissertation and subsequent book. But partly perhaps the discrepancy is also explained by the culture of the 1930s when homosexuality could scarcely be spoken of openly and when there was real fear of scandal about one of Halifax's ancient gentry families. The key to the code came into Edward Green's possession only in 1937, when Muriel Green had completed the most of her work; and, she later recalled, lesbianism 'doesn't come into the letters really - some are rather affectionate . . . but I just thought they were very flowery letters. I didn't realise quite what it was then'[35]

Anne Lister's deceptive mannered style certainly allowed that reading of the letters then. But readers now familiar with Helena Whitbread's two editions of the diaries will want to re-read the Anne Lister letters in this new light. In particular, letters like those to Eliza Raine or Isabella Norcliffe may now be open to a new and different reading.[36] This re-reading suggests, for instance, that Anne's use of romantic and literary conventions masked deeper meanings.

The Letters: Survival or Destruction

Anne Lister and her intimate web of female friends had particular reason to attach considerable significance to the language of letter-writing - and to the process of letter-*keeping*. This is clearly brought out in one of Anne's memoranda written to herself: it offers a vividly reminder that the 1,850 letters which survive in the Shibden Hall Muniments boxes represent only a fraction of a much larger original number of Anne Lister letters. She was a meticulously organised person: when letters were received their date was recorded; they were noted in her diary marginalia and sometimes transcribed into the journals and they were then hoarded in neatly labelled parcels. Indeed, Anne Lister was her own archivist, obsessively sorting her own papers with an eye to what could prudently be preserved. One particular period of reviewing her papers was August 1822, just half-way through her letter-writing life. She had recently written to Mariana. (Mariana Belcombe and Anne Lister had become lovers in 1814 when Anne was twenty three: Mariana's strategic marriage in March 1816 had devastated Anne, but their passionate

relationship continued.[37] Anne now wrote to Mariana: 'Anxiety for your happiness is the high-priest that does the service of my soul. God grant that an affection so deeply rooted - so intensely strong, may be a comfort to us both, and form one bright spot in our lives'.[38])
It was at this point she decided to record a systematic inventory:

Contents of my letter-Drawer
. . . Parcel of letters 9 from S[am]L. to A.L. & 5 from A.L. to S.L. from 1810 to 1813 . . .

Letters

1. Parcel	6 A.L. to I[sabella] N[orcliffe] 1810 . . .
20. —	60 M[ariana] P.B[elcombe] to A.L. } 1812 & 1813 & from A.L. to M.P.B.}
21. —	87 M.P.B. to A.L. }1814 A.L. to M.P.B. . . . }
33. —	12 Partly from Miss M[arsh] partly from Mr D[uffin] respecting E[Liza] R[aine]'s insanity . . .

- Papers concerning M.P.B. 1814 & 1815 }
My journal of our acquaintance . . . }

Pocket book containing memoranda not to be looked at b[u]t [by] A.L.
Racing calendar: Tib's [ie Isabella's] swearing language . . .

Bl[ac]k book given me by M.P.L[awton] 9 February 1816 . . .
Mrs B—'s [Mariana's?] journal of a week in March 1816 . . .
List of Miss [Marsh]'s letters before burning them &
Obs[?erva tions] dated May 1822
Purse & seal from Miss McL[ean] . . .

My deal-box for letters & papers contains several parcels of miscellaneous letters [and] also my mother's, my aunt's, Marian's, E.R—'s, I.N—'s of 1821, & all those . . . respecting my father's estate in Market W[eighton] . . .[39]

It is immediately clear that thirty-one-year-old Anne Lister had

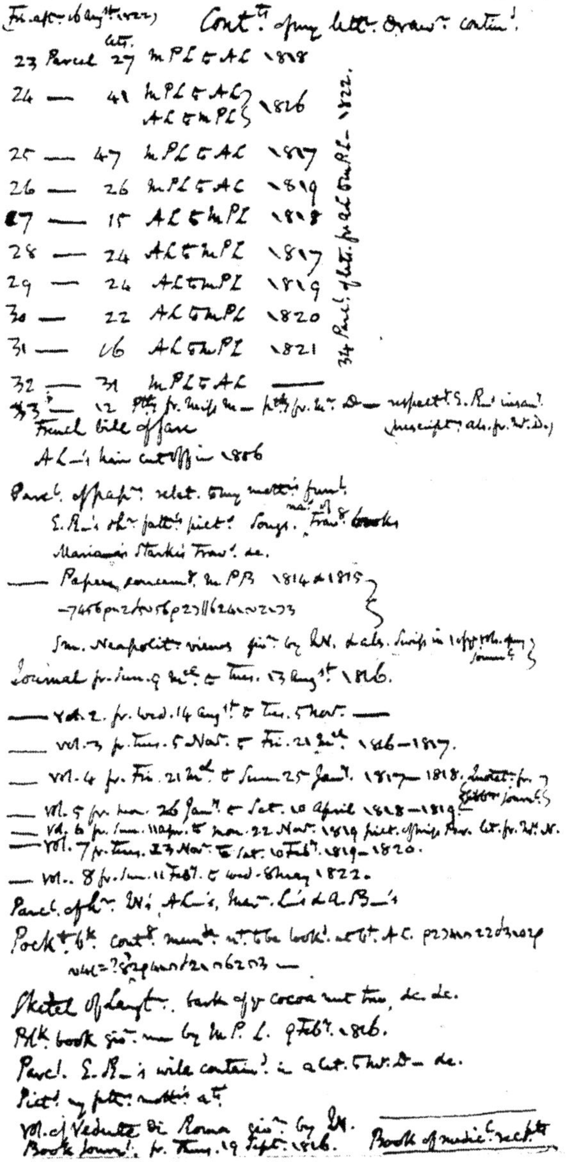
Fri. aftn. 16 Augt. 1822) Cont.ts of my lett. drawr. contin'd.
23 Parcel 27 lett. MPL to AL 1818
24 — 41 MPL to AL / AL to MPL 1826
25 — 47 MPL to AL 1817
26 — 26 MPL to AL 1819
27 — 15 AL to MPL 1818
28 — 24 AL to MPL 1817
29 — 24 AL to MPL 1819
30 — 22 AL to MPL 1820
31 — 16 AL to MPL 1821
32 — 31 MPL to AL —
34 Parcl. of letts. fr. AL to MPL – 1822.
French bill of fare
AL—'s hair cut off in 1806
Journal fr. Sun. 9 Mar. to Tues. 13 Augt. 1816.
— Vol. 2. fr. Wed. 14 Augt. to Tues. 5 Novr. —
— Vol. 3 fr. Tues. 5 Novr. to Fri. 21 Mar. 1816–1817.
— Vol. 4 fr. Fri. 21 Mar. to Sun. 25 Jany. 1817–1818.
— Vol. 5 fr. Mon. 26 Jany. to Sat. 10 April 1818–1819
— Vol. 6 fr. Sun. 11 Apr. to Mon. 22 Novr. 1819
— Vol. 7 fr. Tues. 23 Novr. to Sat. 10 Feby. 1819–1820.
— Vol. 8 fr. Sun. 11 Feby. to Wed. 8 May 1822.
Pock.t book giv. me by MPL. 9 Feby. 1816.
Vol. of Vedute di Roma giv. by IN.
Book Journ'l. fr. Thurs. 19 Sept. 1816.

From the inventory of contents of Anne Lister's letter drawer, 16 August 1822, SH:7/ML/MISC/2/2. By kind permission of Calderdale District Archives.

already burnt some letters - in this case from Miss Marsh, a close friend in York. Clearly too, by 1822, well over four hundred copies between Anne and Mariana had been carefully parcelled up in Anne's letter drawer. But only a handful of items from this loving correspondence survives today in the Shibden Hall Muniments. At some point, hundred of letters were destroyed. When? It is not clear. But in 1850, ten years after Anne's death, her trustees calendared the Muniments; alongside the diaries and the neat books of business letters and accounts, are listed:

> 212 Paper parcel with Private Letters to Mrs Lister . . .
> 215 do do Drafts of [Letters] in Mrs Listers Handwriting . . .
> 217 Paper parcel with Private letters to Mrs Lister & her letters to Miss MacLean.[40]

The absence of references here to Mariana's letters when compared to the 1822 inventory suggests the destruction (probably burning) may well have taken place in the 1830s or 1840s.[41] By whom? A prudently methodical Anne Lister in the 1830s? An insanely jealous Ann Walker in the 1840s? Although it is difficult to be precise yet about exactly what happened, it provides a reminder that at a time when photography was in its infancy, the chance of someone stumbling upon a letter remained a powerful fear about the discovery of evidence pointing to a relationship not fully recognised by polite society.[42]

Anne Lister's journals survived the one hundred and fifty years since they were written more successfully than her correspondence, where possibly about twice the number of letters originally existed. So it is upon the diaries themselves (or lengthy extracts of letters copied into the diaries) that we must largely rely to reconstruct Anne and Mariana's relationship. The pitifully few surviving letters come mainly from the 1830s, and only occasionally suggest how close remained the twenty-year affair - such as a copy of a letter written by Anne in October 1834 about an earlier misunderstanding:

> My dearest Mary . . .there has ever been a film across your eyes to me; . . . you have feared where no fear was - you have

> doubted where no doubt ought to have been . . . I say, & think, you determined wisely for us both, because our happiness together was become too difficult. Remember how you yourself despaired of it, from the time of our ill-fated journey to Holland [in 1831] . . . But God bless you, Mary! I can serve you better now than I could have done before . . .[43]

Anne Lister: Businesswoman

An equally significant cache of Anne Lister correspondence is her three notebooks containing nearly five hundred drafts of business letters written by her 1826-1838. These were addressed to the professional or commercial men paid to perform a specific service for Anne or her Shibden estate. These letters fall into three main categories. First, Anne wrote regularly to local Halifax men like Robert Parker and his partner Adam, the family solicitors, about estate business (such as the land transaction letter quoted earlier); the local bank manager, her estate steward David Booth or the local Tory election committee agent. Second, at a county level, Anne wrote to York men such as John Harper, the architect supervising her Shibden 'improvements' and Grays, the old-established attorneys who handled her will and major financial transactions.[44] Third, at a national level, Anne wrote to men in London such as her bankers, Hammersleys, who arranged her passports and foreign travel, and to other London (or occasionally French or Swiss) tradesmen for goods, services and the hiring of servants.[45] As suggested earlier, this buzz of business letters clearly confirms that Anne Lister was well respected by her male peers as a very hard-headed negotiator who would always drive a tough bargain. Even while travelling in distant Russia, she chose to keep a very close rein on David Booth, left responsible for running the adjoining estates while she and Ann Walker travelled:

> Moscow, Tuesday 17 December 1839
>
> Booth -
> I have received all Mr Parker's letters. It was right to send

me a copy of the letter you sent off on the 10th of August but which has not reached me . . . Go on writing in the same way, except that you had best put all concerning Miss Walker by itself, and all concerning me by itself, so that one part can be torn off from the other.

I am very anxious about the colliery: but, as I shall not be at home for some months, and as I am sure no care and attention will be wanting on your part, I shall, in the mean time, leave you to manage as well as you can, according to the orders already given; and I merely repeat, that no expenses must be incurred which can be well avoided, and that, if you cannot keep the water down with the pumps as you now have, you must stop the works . . .

Look well after the stone quarries. Let me know if times are tolerable, if there is much spirit for building in the town - if the Northgate hotel is going on well, and if coal is likely to sell well, and to keep up in price, or not . . .

Tell me what you have made by the farm, and what the horses have earned by coal-carting. Tell John to see there is great plenty of strawberries - to take care of the asparagus beds, and to plant some Jerusalem artichokes.

I am &c &c &c

A. Lister.[46]

Anne Lister had little trouble wielding stern authority in the predominantly male world of estate management. She was as willing as any other Halifax colliery owner to exploit the narrow coal seams beneath her estate to ensure a profit. But by the late 1830s, was her world - that of the independent female member of the minor landed gentry - passing? Davidoff and Hall's influential *Family Fortunes: Men and women of the English middle class 1780-1850* describes how increased specialization in agriculture disadvantaged such women entrepreneurs:

There was a growing feeling that genteel women . . . should be removed from contact with [day labourers] . . . With a predominantly male workforce, it was even more difficult for

> women to wield authority . . .
>
> These factors bore particularly heavily on women operating in their own right . . . In addition to dealing with a wage labour force, there were also clients, bankers, solicitors and agents. These would be men with increasingly fixed expectations of appropriate feminine behaviour . . .
>
> Within this pattern, certain activities became more closely associated with one or other gender . . . The equation of outdoor activity with men, and indoors as the setting for respectable femininity affected the division of labour in a myriad of ways.[47]

Certainly, the unconventional Anne Lister and her gentry friends no longer seem to fit the image of early nineteenth century bourgeois women delineated by Davidoff and Hall:

> Women cultivated the language of friendship and love in which sexual passion had no part. (Thomas Bowdler's expurgated *Family Shakespeare* was published in 1818.) By the early nineteenth century, there had been a gradual shift from the earlier view of women as sexually voracious towards the innocence and passivity of Victorian sensibility . . . Seduction and adultery, the speciality of the debauched gentry, were severely censured.[48]

Anne Lister and her lesbian network of friends managed to elude severe censure, partly through their ancient gentry class credentials and partly through exercising discretion: her correspondence at one level certainly reads as a model of discreet writing. And once she became independent and well-travelled businesswoman, running her estate and making decisions in her own right, how many would dare to censure her openly?

Reading - and Re-Reading - Across the Documents

What then is the value of the Anne Lister letters balanced against the diaries and their coded passages? Are the four-million-word journals and their code *still* the jewel in the Anne Lister crown?

Probably they are. For to read the diaries is to begin to read the correspondence; whereas a reading of the correspondence on its own demands a re-reading in the light of the diaries - partly to discover the context in which a letter was written, and partly to check how many other letters were exchanged at the time but have since been destroyed or lost. The journals record almost obsessively Anne Lister's ceaseless letter-writing. Indeed, the very earliest diary - for August 1806 - opens as an inventory of the daily correspondence exchanged between Anne and Eliza Raine. Later, when her journal-writing becomes more systematic (with marginal signs indicating a note or a letter exchanged), sending, receiving and copying letters to her key correspondents continues to shape the daily diary. Indeed, by the 1830s many pages of the journal are filled with Anne's transcription of letters exchanged - particularly with Mariana Lawton.

But the value of the letters should not be underestimated. First they have a particular richness because each represents a relationship: between Anne and her friends, her lovers, her sister and her aunt, her solicitors and steward. Given the practical problems in reading a four-million-word diary, roughly a sixth of which is in code, the correspondence offers a shorter guide to Anne's life. It helps sort Anne's key relationships into broad - albeit sometimes overlapping - groupings: family, friendships, sexual, business and political relationships. Read alongside the diaries, the letters confirm, for instance, that lesbianism is a crucial theme in understanding Anne Lister - but is not the only theme.

Second, the language Anne Lister uses in her correspondence is more richly varied than the writing in her journals. This might be expected. A person's daily diary is an intimate record but a matter-of-fact record. It is not the place to deploy mannered figures of speech and elaborate rhetorical flourishes. Letters can be. Anne Lister's correspondence lends itself to readings and re-readings in the light of what is now revealed in the diaries (and other manuscript material). The style Anne chose to present to her correspondents indicates vividly the precise quality of each of Anne Lister's complex relationships. The peremptory tone used to issue David Booth with instructions about the estate is telling evidence of the deference the gentry might exact from a steward, and contrasts starkly with the affectionate tone Anne adopted towards Mariana, the playful teasing of Isabella or the guile underlying letters to Ann Walker.

Linked to this, the surviving letters allow us to read the public face that Anne Lister chose to present to her correspondents, a face less visible in the confessional private world of a diary. The careful keeping of drafts or copies of letters to Lady Stuart or to Maria Barlow tells us much about what Anne Lister really cared about; and the regular sorting and burning of personal letters indicates what she really feared in the public sphere.

In other words, to come as close as possible to Anne Lister in any given period, it is necessary to read *across* the documents - from diary to letters, from letters to other manuscript material. One example illustrates this: in the 1832 parliamentary election, Anne's diary records how she actively coerced tenants like farmer John Bottomley into voting for the Tory candidate and how she sent for Bottomley 'to tell him to vote for Wortley tomorrow'. But what we gain from reading across from the diary to the business correspondence is a copy of the letter actually sent by a trusty intermediary to Bottomley telling him how to vote, prefaced by a curt note: 'Wrote & gave him [the intermediary] the following to be torn up on J.B-'s having read it'.[49]

* * *

The Anne Lister manuscripts are a complex and tortuous labyrinth, full of perplexing tunnels. What the searcher needs is a map or guide to indicate the dimensions of all these dark passages. Researchers feeling their way into the maze will soon discover that the passages are interconnected; that the correspondence can act as an invaluable guide to the four-million word diary; and that the other manuscript material provides important links to both.[50] Earlier editors of the diaries have provided invaluable threads to follow. But perhaps the methodical signposting by Muriel Green in the 1930s deserves particular appreciation. Her professional librarian's listing and transcribing half-a-century ago of so many of the letters have left contemporary Anne Lister scholars in her debt. The serious work on the Anne Lister manuscripts now beginning is in large part thanks to Muriel Green's pioneering achievement. It allows the historian to read - and to re-read - across the documents for particular themes or periods in order come as close as possible to the real Anne Lister and to open up to view the full richness of the Anne Lister manuscript material.

Notes

These two articles, which first appeared in 1993 in *History Workshop Journal* and the *Transactions of the Halifax Antiquarian Society*, are reprinted here without any major alteration. The only changes made have been to ensure that *Presenting the Past* avoids repetitions. Thus the titles of the two articles have been simplified; the *History Workshop Journal* style of references and abbreviations has been adapted for both articles; page numbering has been made consistent, and subheadings added to the second article. Additionally, a few minor changes to the text have been made - particularly concerning the letters, where the exact dimensions of the Anne Lister correspondence and its relationship to the letters Anne transcribed into her diaries are only now becoming clear.

'Re-reading the Correspondence' began as a review of Muriel Green's 1992 book but, as the fullness of the Shibden Hall letters collection became more apparent, it developed into a longer and more analytical study of the Anne Lister correspondence.

Guide to References and Abbreviations

AL:	Anne Lister diaries (SH:7/ML/E/1-24 & 26).
HG:	John Lister (ed), 'Some Extracts from the Diary of a Halifax Lady,' *Halifax Guardian* (1887-92).
HW (1988):	Helena Whitbread (ed), *I Know My Own Heart: The Diaries of Anne Lister 1791-1840*, Virago Press, London 1988.
HW (1992)	Helena Whitbread (ed), *No Priest but Love: The Journals of Anne Lister from 1824-1826*, Smith Settle, Otley 1992.
MG (1938):	Muriel Green, 'A Spirited Yorkshirewoman: The Letters of Anne Lister of Shibden Hall, Halifax b.1791-d.1840', Library Association Honours Diploma, 1938.
MG (1992)	Muriel Green (ed), *Miss Lister of Shibden Hall: Selected Letters (1800-1840)*, Book Guild, Lewes 1992.
SH:	Shibden Hall Muniments (Calderdale Archives).
RAM:	Phyllis Ramsden papers (Calderdale Archives).
THAS:	*Transactions of the Halifax Antiquarian Society*.

Anne Lister of Shibden Hall: Her Diaries and the Historians

1 Recent books suggested Welton, but SH:3/LF/28/5 states Halifax.

2 D. Lang, 'Georgia in 1840: the Lister Diaries', *THAS* 1989.

3 David Ward, *Guardian,* 17.2.1984.

4 Full publication details are given in *Abbreviations* above. HW(1992) was published after this article was written, shortly before it went to press.

5 My own word count, autumn 1990, using microfilm copies of diaries. The three earliest volumes had somehow come adrift. (Strictly speaking, there are 26 volumes plus early loose fragments; but I refer to them here as 27.)

6 Of 226 boxes, 27 contain Anne Lister mss; for instance, the Shibden collection contains about half-a-dozen diaries.

7 SH:7/ML/MISC/9 is unclear whether AL travelled with all her diaries, or left the earlier volumes in a drawer at home. Household census, 6.6.1841, Southowram township; also six servants.

8 SH:1/SH/1836/2 is 31 dense pages of legalese and codicils.

9 MAC:73/23, Calderdale Archives, Belcombe to Parker, 8.9.1843.

10 MAC:73/29, Calderdale Archives, Parker memorandum, 9.9.1843.

11 1851 household census, 14 inhabitants included a coal agent, farmer, dressmaker and stone delver; also SH:7/DRL/47.

12 SH:3/LAW/41/3; SH:7/DRL/48.

13 Also Wilkie Collins *The Woman in White* 1860 about 'mad' women and inheritance.

14 SH:3/L/93; 'Mrs' is a courtesy title.

15 An example of the official myth is Calderdale Leisure Services, *Shibden Hall: Halifax* (n.d.), 'Shibden Hall Families', p 4. See SH:3/LAW/42/1, SH:7/JN/243 etc for other attempted claims to Shibden.

16 Ben Wilson, a Halifax Chartist, *Newspaper Cuttings*, Halifax Library, 'Halifax 60 Years Ago and the Progress It has Made': Anne Lister 'was tall, and in her features and walk was much like a man, and was very eccentric in her ways and dress'.

17 Emily Brontë taught at Law Hill near Shibden c 1838, and very likely knew of Anne Lister; see W Gérin, *Emily Brontë: A Biography,* 1971, p 74. Charlotte died in 1855.

18 Lillian Faderman, *Surpassing the Love of Men: Romantic Friendship and Love between Women from the Renaissance to the Present*, Junction Books, London 1981, p 154. For recent criticism of this pioneering book see, for instance, Martin Duberman, Martha Vicinus and George Chauncey (eds) *Hidden from History: Reclaiming the Gay and Lesbian Past*, 1989 Penguin 1991, p. 4 - 7.

19 Rosa Kettle, *The Mistress of Langdale Hall*, Tinsley, 1872, pp 20, 29, 94, 112.

20 The total word length is about 240,000, of which perhaps 20% is editorial and genealogical matter or is taken from AL's letters.

21 SH:7/ML/E/25, *Halifax Guardian*, p 1.

22 *HG,* LXVII

23 Further research on the Shibden Hall mss is much needed here.

24 Eg *HG,* XXXII, XLVII.

25 Burrell was a classics scholar who taught at Bradford Grammar School 1881-99; he refers to the incident both as 'some fifty years ago' and as 'forty years at least', or c. 1886 to c. 1894. My own hunch is around 1892, but it may have been later.

Thanks to Alan Betteridge whose reclassification of this mss in 1992 brought its significance to light, allowing me to piece together the story for the final draft of this article. Previously the cracking of the code was shrouded in mystery, and was thought to have taken place about the 1920s.

26 SH:7/JN/B/74/6 & 7 (12 & 20.12.1936).

27 Faderman, Surpassing, pp 239-52; J Weeks, *Coming Out: Homosexual Politics in Britain from the Nineteenth Century to the Present*, Quartet, London 1977, chaps 2-6; Krafft-Ebing's *Psychopathia Sexualis* was published in London in 1892. However, debate continues on the influence of the sexologists, see Duberman etc (eds), *Hidden,* pp. 4 & 213.

Local people later reminisced about John Lister's homosexuality, though is only hinted at in H Drake, 'John Lister of Shibden Hall (1847-1933): First Treasurer of the Independent Labour Party', Ph D, University of Bradford [c. 1972], pp. x-xxii, 170, noting his isolation and melancholy.

28 Interview recorded with Muriel Green, 18.9.1991, p. 1: See p.50.

29 Interview with Muriel Green, p 3.

30 SH:7/JN/B/74/7 and 8 (20.12.1936 and 1.1.1937). Burrell died in 1946.

31 Interview, pp. 3-4; Muriel Green, 'The Shibden Hall Muniments', *THAS,* 1938, p. 70.

32 For discussion of the AL letters, see 'Anne Lister of Shibden Hall: Re-reading the Correspondence', pp. 48-66.

33 For instance, MG (1938) p. 79 and MG (1992) p. 33.

34 For instance, M E Kendall, 'Miss Lister's Diary: Extracts and Comments', *THAS*, 1950; *THAS* 'Pedigree of Lister of Shibden Hall' 1956. An undated anonymous typescript biography 'The Life of Anne Lister of Halifax 1791-1840' was also written about this time.

35 V. Ingham, 'Anne Lister in the Pyrenees', *THAS*, 1969, p. 55.

36 Phyllis Ramsden, 'Anne Lister's Journal (1817-1840), *THAS* , 1970, p.1.

37 RAM:47, Museums Director to Ramsden, 17.7.1958.

38 RAM: 53, volume 1 (Ramsden gives Mariana's husband as D- rather than C-).

39 RAM: 61, diary vol. 9. See also HW (1992) pp. 148-50.

40 RAM: 60, volume 8, Oct 1824 - March 1825; handwritten note 'March 1966'. See HW (1992) pp. 24 - 90.

41 RAM: 48, 50, 51 (20.7.1964, 18.8.1964, 9.10.1964); the archive service was created 1.4.1964.

42 Ingham, *THAS* 1969, p. 55. Interview with Muriel Green, pp. 3, 5.

43 Ramsden, *THAS*, pp 4, 10-11.

44 RAM: 8, p 2; RAM: 6-46.

45 RAM: 6, p 3; RAM: 7, p 4; RAM: 28, p. 9.

46 *Halifax Courier*, 11.9.1985 and 23.2.1988; her remaining papers are in Calderdale Archives. The *Guardian* article included interviews with both Ramsden and historian Dorothy Thompson. Dorothy Thompson, who had earlier lived in Halifax, was among the Yorkshire scholars long interested in AL and familiar with John Lister's transcription. See for instance D. Thompson, 'Women, Work and Politics in Nineteenth-Century England: the problem of authority' in J. Rendall (ed), *Equal or Different: Women's Politics 1800-1914,* Blackwell, Oxford 1987, p. 76. (See also endnote 55)

47 The main volumes were microfilmed in 1982, and the earliest volumes in 1990. Thanks to Alan Betteridge for his help in piecing together the transmission story.

John Wain, *The Journals of James Boswell 1760-1795*, Heinemann 1991, Introduction, which summarizes a complex tale of family censorship and the retrieval of four caches of manuscript material.

48 HW (1988), p. xii and HW (1992) p. xi.

49 HW (1988), pp. 128, 53, 263.

50 *Halifax Courier*, 29.1.1988; eg HW (1988) pp. 273, 297.

51 HW (1988), p 237.

52 Angela John, *Gender and History*, vol 1 no 1, spring 1989, p 112; thanks to Linda Walker.

53 HW (1988) p. xii; *Halifax Courier*, 6 and 23.2.1988; verbal comment was stronger.

54 MG (1992) remains reticent to acknowledge AL's lesbianism, eg p. 73 'virus' reference.

Whitbread (1992) p. xi does acknowledge John Lister's cracking of the code, but does not note his transcript and does not mention Ramsden or Green. (See also note 87.)

55 In 1986 Dorothy Thompson, then teaching history at Birmingham University, received a 2-year ESRC grant to fund transcription of the diaries from microfilm copies. The 1986-88 Birmingham project completed a handwritten transcript of roughly 600,000 words (ie about 15% of the whole) mainly of the 1817-21 period. I would like to thank Dorothy Thompson for all her help here.

Patricia Hughes, the project Research Associate, who undertook the transcript, is currently working on a life of Eliza Raine, 'A Lady of Colour'. For further on Raine, see pp. 28-30.

56 7.10.1989; Pauline Millward's talk on 'diaries are dangerous things' included discussion of Peterloo.

57 ESRC, 8.5.1991; see note 55 above.

58 Earlier drafts of this article included a short fourth section on AL in Russia (5-

10.2.1840); but for reasons of space this had to be omitted. The main theme under-represented is therefore AL's travel.

As there is not space here to reproduce the three sections in their entirety, readers have for the moment to take my selections from them on trust. There is also little reference here to the correspondence and other AL manuscript material; see 'Re-reading the Correspondence', pp.48-66.

59 SH:7/ML/E/26/1; this also includes about 4,500 words of additional loose pages 1810 -14, mainly in code and mainly about poor Isabella Norcliffe. There are serious problems of pagination and dating here.

60 MG (1938), p. 210; SH:7/ML/13 (1805).

61 AL 23.11.1808; 21.3.1809.

62 AL, 8.5.1809; also AL, 27.11.1806, 21.10.1808, 20, 27.3.1809.

63 AL, 28.10 and 28.12.1806; also 23.11.1807, 3.4.1808 and 25.5.1808.

64 From 30.6.1808 the word *'felix'* (Latin = happy, fruitful) dots the pages of the diary during ER's visit; ER's own diary (SH:7/ML/A/14) includes a note (2.8-8.11.1808) in which the word *'Felix'* is similarly used.

65 AL, 28.10 and 9.11.1808; there is a gap in diary text between 5.7.1809 and 15.1.1810.

66 SH:7/ML/A/14 (7.7.1809 and 18.12.1809).

67 AL, 16.1.1810.

68 SH:7/ML/A/14.

69 It seems there is a long gap in the diaries, plus a missing volume.

70 MG (1938), p. 12; RAM: 52; HW (1988) pp. x, 369; HW (1992) pp. 4-6 helpfully illuminates these early years.

71 Faderman, *Surpassing* p. 147-52, one law lord adding 'there is no indecency in one woman going to bed with another'; also pp. 120-43 on the Ladies of Llangollen. Terry Castle's review of Faderman's *Scotch Verdict*, *Signs* summer 1984, pp. 717-20, suggests interesting parallels with the Manor School.

72 HW (1988), p 210. The tangled sexual world revealed by AL's diaries makes interesting comparison with Carroll Smith-Rosenberg's classic study, 'The Female World of Love and Ritual: Relations between Women in Nineteenth-Century America', *Signs* 1: 1,1975.

73 SH:7/ML/E/3; the transcript covers 1-31.8.1809, 1-3 and 10-20.9.1809 and 1-8.10.1809.

74 AL, 3.9.1819.

75 AL, 28.8 and 13.9.1819.

76 AL, 4.8.1819.

77 *Commercial Directory for 1818, 19, & 20*, pp 140-48.

78 E. Thompson, *The Making of the English Working Class*, (1963) Pelican, 1968, p. 754, also p. 663.

79 AL, 16 and 17.8.1819.

80 AL, 16, 17 and 18.8.1819.

81 AL, 19 and 24.8.1819.

82 AL, 5 and 8.10.1819.

83 AL, 27.8.1819.

84 AL, 13.8.1819; also 3 and 19.8.1819. For one interpretation of 'kiss', see HW (1988) p 368.

85 Possibly this distancing from West Riding's turbulent past was because Peterloo meant less to his generation, or because of his own local patrotism. For background on local Liberal optimism, see E P Thompson's introduction to Frank Peel, *The Rising of the Luddites*, 1968, pp vii-ix.

86 RAM: 55; Muriel Green alone cites the diary for Peterloo.

87 HW (1988), p. 103; also 100-1 and 107-8. In a 4-week sample (3-30.8.1819), the coded passages at this period comprise about 23% of the diary, and about 41% in HW (1988).

88 However, for publication the non-Peterloo sections may well need a firm editorial hand.

89 SH:7/ML/E/15; transcription covers 1-8, 16-19, (partial) 22-24, 25-29.9.1832; and 1-14.12.1832.

90 Will (at Borthwick Institute, York) signed 3.8.1822.

91 See HW (1992) pp. 204-5.

92 *HG,* LXXXVIII (13.10.1834).

93 AL, 16.12.1832.

94 Thanks very much to this Helena Whitbread for this information.

95 MG (1938), p 435; also *HG,* XCXI, (9.8.1837). This is another area needing more work.

96 AL, 11.12.1832.

97 *The Poll Book*, Halifax 1833, p 1;

98 Quoted in J. A. Jowitt, 'Parliamentary Politics in Halifax, 1832-1847', *Northern History*, 1976.

99 AL, 16.12.1832.

100 AL, 2, 3 and 5.9.1832; AL used a cross in the margin; thanks to Helena Whitbread for this point.

101 AL, 27.9.1832; 'moil' meant 'drudgery' but was later used to mean 'turmoil'.

102 AL, 28.9.1832.

103 AL, 8.12.1832; 'grubble' (which perhaps also included caress or fondle) was obsolete by 1719, according to the *SOED*.

104 AL, 14.12.1832.

105 For instance, 13.12.1832 at Lidgate ends with Ann Walker's reading prayers to the servants, and 14.12.1832 opens with *'pressing and lovemaking till after three this morning'*.

106 MG (1932), p 438; RAM: 67.

107 *HG,* XCIX (17.7.1837). See pp.54-62 for AL 1833-40.

108 Joan Perkin, *Women and Marriage in Nineteenth-century England*, Routledge 1989, pp 90, 51-2.

109 See F.M.L. Thompson, *English Landed Society in the Nineteenth Century*, Routledge, London 1963, pp. 256-68.

110 *HG,* LXXXIX (3.12.1834).

111 Leonore Davidoff and Catherine Hall, *Family Fortunes: Men and Women of the English middle class 1780-1850*, Hutchinson 1987, eg pp. 401-2, 274-5. Thanks to Cat Euler for discussion here.

112 Faderman, *Surpassing,* p 254 ff describes a Paris sub-culture; Halifax is a less obvious site for bohemian homosexuality.

113 MG (1992), p 17; Ramsden, *Guardian,* 17.2.1984; HW (1988) p.xii.

114 Michael Foucault, *The History of Sexuality*, (1976) Penguin1979, eg p. 35, 'What is peculiar to modern societies, in fact, is not that they consigned sex to a shadowy existence, but that they dedicated themselves to speaking about it *ad infinitum*, while exploiting it as *the* secret'.

115 They indicate that early 19th century lesbian relations could be sexual and genital, rather than just 'romantic friendships'. Smith-Rosenberg, 'Female World' makes interesting comparison here. Based upon the correspondence and diaries of women and men in thirty-five middle-class American families between the 1760s and 1880s, it depicts a world of female intimacy similar to that of Anne Lister, of gossip-filled letters, gift exchange, diary-keeping, and of 'that endless trooping of women into each others' homes for social purposes . . . at times even dislodging husbands from their beds and bedrooms so that dear friends might spend every hour of every day together'. But while Anne rejected heterosexual marriage completely and had no interest at all in domesticity, for Smith-Rosenberg, daughters were born into a female world, central to which was the traditional domestic apprenticeship of daughter to mother.

Lisa Moore, ' "Something more tender still than friendship": romantic friendship in early-nineteenth century England', *Feminist Studies*, vol.18, no.3, Fall 1992, offers a valuable critique of the pioneering studies of both Smith-Rosenberg and Lillian Faderman and 'their reliance on the category of gender to the exclusion of a systematic consideration of sexuality'.

116 For instance, P. Millward, 'Will the real Anne Lister please stand up!', *Ad Lib*, Calderdale Libraries 1992, contrasting HW (1988) and MG (1992): 'it would be difficult to discover two more disparate portraits . . . these disparities do raise the question as to whether the subject herself is the same!'

117 HW (1992), p. xii, is much more open about the problems. 'It seemed to me that Anne ought to tell her own story before anyone interpreted it for her . . . My decision to give Anne Lister's love story to the world was not taken either lightly or from reasons of prurience . . . My chosen theme, then, was the long-running love affair between Anne Lister and Marianna Lawton . . .' (Editors have offered various spellings for M—'s name, but 'Mariana' is given as her signature in eg, SH:7/ML/703.)

Anne Lister of Shibden Hall
Re-reading the Correspondence

1. HW (1988) and HW(1992). Please see p.67 for Guide to References and Abbreviations.

2 See pp. 7-47.

3 MG (1992).

4 Even more compact is P. Ramsden, 'Anne Lister's Journal (1817-1840)', *THAS*, 1970, which represents a major landmark in AL research; see p.20-1.

5 MG (1992) pp. 27-8 & 199-202.

6 MG (1938).

7 See pp.10-12 for a brief summary of this litigation.

8 'Pedigree of Lister of Shibden Hall', *THAS* ,1956.

9 J. Robinson, 'Index of Transactions by Year and by Author 1901-1990', *HAS;* it is unlikely that John Lister published further studies on AL elsewhere. For the cracking of the code, see pp. 14-5.

10 The park was given by A.C.McCrae in 1923; he acquired the reversion of Shibden Hall for the borough who received its ownership in 1933. Thanks to Ros Westwood for this note.

11 M. Green, 'History in Letters: the Cataloguing and Arranging of Collections of Family Letters', *Library Association Record,* February 1937, p. 1.

12 Interview recorded by writer, 18.9.1991, p 1. The list of John Lister's books, 148 typed single-spaced foolscap pages, was produced by Halifax Libraries in 1935 .

13 Green, '*History in Letters*', p. 2.

14 Interview, p 3.

15 M. Green F.L.A., 'A Woman in Advance of Her Times: The Letters of Anne Lister of Shibden Hall. Born 1791 - Dies 1840', *Halifax Courier and Guardian,* 4.4 - 27.6.1936.

16 M. Green, 'The Shibden Hall Muniments', *THAS* 1938.

17 Dissertation total length probably approximately 300,000 words, of which roughly 250,000 is transcription. Figures given here for the number of 'letters' are necessarily approximate; and AL's 'letters' varied between notes of a few words to book-length travelogues.

18 MG (1938), p 50 (13.4.1811 - SH:7/ML/41). Sam died by drowning in 1813.

19 MG (1938), 22-23; (21.7.1810 - SH/7/ML/27. Carroll Smith-Rosenberg, 'The Female World of Love and Ritual: Relations between Women in Nineteenth-Century America', *Signs* autumn 1975, pp 8 & 27 uses the term 'romantic rhetoric'.

20 AL had studied classical rhetoric; see SH:7/ML/MISC/2/2

21 See also P. Millward, 'Will the real Anne Lister please stand up!', *Ad Lib* Calderdale Libraries, December 1992, comparing Whitbread's 1988 portrait with Green's 1992 one and concluding, 'it would be difficult to discover two more disparate portraits . . . these disparities do raise the question as to whether the subject herself is the same!'

22 There are approximately 1,850 letters in the SH:7/ML collection in Calderdale District Archives. In addition, there are a few in other collections (eg, local solicitors' papers), and a handful in the Chancery Masters' Exhibits, Public Record Office.

23 Calderdale District Archives 'Shibden Hall Muniments', November 1983, SH:7/ML - SH:7/ML/MISC. The exact evolution of the catalogue 1938-70 is unclear; thanks to Alan Betteridge for all his help on this point.

24 The writing here is probably a mixture of Green's and post-war hands.

25 There are only about 1,285 catalogue cards in the SH:7/ML & SH:7/ML/A-D drawers. This discrepancy is largely because SH:7/ML/C (draft business letters) is represented by just three cards (for the three notebooks containing these drafts) but in fact comprises roughly 483 separate items. (Also, a few cards cover more than one item of correspondence.),

26 See Green 'History in Letters', p. 1, for discussion of envelopes, postmarks, sealing wax etc..

27 A further dozen concern the family pedigree.

28 Most are in SH:7/ML/C, but there are also some in SH:7/ML.

29 SH:7/ML/C/3 p 99.

30 See pages 71-2, note 115.

31 14.3.1833 - SH:7/ML/664; quoted in MG (1938), p.438.

32 RAM:68 (1967), 10.2.1833.

33 SH:7/ML/854/2 (13.6.1835).

34 Chancery Masters' Exhibits (C106/60), 27.2.1835 notes, PRO.

35 Interview, p 4,

36 Thanks to Tom Steele for discussion on reading and re-reading.

37 HW (1992) pp 5-6.

38 John Lister, XLVII (July 1822).

39 SH:7/ML/MISC/2/2, 16-27.8.1822; also parcel wrapping paper has been preserved! Also 'Contents of my Canteen', similar date, for objects; also AL, 16.8.1822.

40 SH:3/L/93; thanks to Julian Harber for his help here.

41 References to Anne's letter-burning include MG (1938), pp. 43, 46, 185 & 196. Anne and Mariana were still writing to each other at least once a week in the early 1830s; for instance, in the first four months of 1833, they exchanged about eighteen letters.

42 For instance, C. Brontë, *Villette,* 1853, notes how duplicate keys were surreptitiously made to open Lucy Snow's locked drawers in order to read her letters; to avoid such prying, Lucy later buries her letters in a sealed bottle.

43 SH:7/ML/807 (5.10.1834)

If about 1,850 Anne Lister letters survive, how many were there originally? It is hazardous to guess, but one possible indication is to compare diary references about notes and letters sent or received over a given period with the number of letters apparently now surviving. Sample months from different periods of her life vary, with a higher proportion surviving once her business correspondence grew. About twice the number of letters (ie nearly four thousand) may well have originally existed.

44 Further research is required into the considerable sums of money involved.

45 Anne and her correspondents relied heavily on each other for information about servants.

46 SH:7/ML/1092; also MG (1938) pp 519- 20; attached was a separate (but similar) letter to David Booth from Ann Walker concerning Shibden-Mill collieries and 'Colliery-tenants', but also including Christmas philanthropy (furniture in the school house, payment to the Lightcliffe Church singers, 'William Green's Xmas shirt which the kitchen girls will make' and ensuring that 'Widow Holt is to have her half-crown as usual'.

Poor David Booth had had to develop a 'journal-like way of writing' to his two employers in Russia, and SH:7/ML/1096 is a copy of an 11-page dossier dated 10.8.1839 (doubtless the one Anne Lister refers to above) chronicling his every daily action and including detailed accounts for the Listerwick Colliery, tenants' annual rents on their cottages and for church pew rents

47 L. Davidoff and C. Hall, *Family Fortunes: Men and women of the English middle class 1780-1850* Hutchinson 1987, pp. 274-5. However, further research on small-scale West Riding farms and on the negotiating of contrasting gentry and middle-class female identities is required here.

48 Davidoff and Hall, *Family Fortunes* pp. 401-2. See also M. J. Peterson, *Family, Love, and Work in the Lives of Victorian Gentlewomen,* Indiana University Press 1989; unfortunately it ignores *Family Fortunes,* published in 1987.

Since the first edition was published in 1994, the literature here has been extensive – for instance, Amanda Vickery, 'Golden Age to Separate Spheres? A review of the categories and chronology of English women's history', *The Historical Journal*, vol. 36, no. 2, 1993. Other key titles can be found in the bibliography of *Female Fortune: Land, Gender and Authority: the Anne Lister Diaries and Other Writings*, 1833-36 (Rivers Oram, 1998).

49 WYAS, CDA, SH:7/ML/C/2, (13.12.1832); see also p.39-40.

50 Thanks to Cat Euler for discussion of the Lister labyrinth. Probably the best example of where the letters act as a crucial guide to the daunting diaries is the last two volumes, together nearly half-a-million words long.

Index